CONTENTS

CHAPTER 1 – BLOOD, SWEAT AND ARREARS

'Behind every great dancer, is a dedicated parent'

And so, the time has arrived, the most poignant of moments, when a chapter of my life comes to its most natural of endings, its completion, concluding, as my Little Princess, my best friend, my daughter, undertakes an exciting progression, a new challenge, as she seeks to make the bold transition from dance student to a career within the industry, as a professional dancer.

The little acorn transforming into the big oak tree, strong enough to stand alone, stable enough to withstand the heavy gusts of wind that the industry holds the potential to deliver.

But, in truth, there lies a slight irrelevance around the ability to stand alone, given that she has no need to, twelve years ago I stood beside her as she took the very first step on her dance journey, and since then, together, we have walked hand in hand along that path, sharing the adventure as a formidable team, and even on reaching this juncture, nothing changes, she is not taking this next step alone, she has no need to, she has me, at the foot of the ladders, holding, offering stability, as she climbs, rung by rung.

You see, I'll always be there, in the background, on call, no matter how far away she might be, whichever far flung corner of the world she might find herself, I'll always be, just one call away. As I always have, as I always will be, to offer help and advice, to deliver guidance and support, forever adapting to those ever changing needs, those new challenges.

I was once told;

> 'With little girls, come little problems, and
> with big girls, come big problems'

Now, substitute the word 'problems' with 'challenges', and that kind of summarises it best.

Years ago, the challenge was learning how to put her hair into a bun, now it's mastering the grand complexities of a self-assessment tax form.

Standing here now, at this crossroads, one that I find to be such a defining moment, holding both the contrasting emotions of sadness and excitement, in equal amounts; looking forwards, to the exciting prospects and opportunities that would hopefully lie ahead, whilst allowing, a more than fleeting glance back over a shoulder, reminiscing on the memories of those fun filled, formative years.

All in all, I have to say, it's been a twelve year journey of highs, lows and just about everything in between, a true tale of;

> 'Blood, sweat and arrears'

Any parent will tell you, having a daughter in the family is an expensive hobby in itself. Allow me to elaborate on that bold statement. I ask you to imagine, envisage, picture the scene;

You're in a secluded wooded area, surrounded by a forest of snow coated trees, the air is crisp, fresh, you're nestled safely inside a log cabin that boasts auld time character, solid wooden beams line the ceiling, a thick fluffy rug lays over the hard stone flooring. Gentle movements, forward, and back on a classic, antique rocking chair. Soft creaks with every movement, as you gaze, almost hypnotically, relaxing in front of an open log fire.

The warm glow, gently caressing your cheeks, the sound of crackling embers filling the room, gentle orchestral music, playing softly in the background.

And you sit there, tossing wads of bank notes, aimlessly, into those scorching flames!

And that is what it is like, a pleasant, highly enjoyable experience, but alas, one that comes with a hefty price tag.

Now take a daughter, and then throw a pair of ballet shoes and a tutu at them, and you'll soon find yourself, logging onto eBay, advertising a kidney for sale!

I suspect in time, evolution will progress and Dance Dads will be born with around twelve kidneys and maybe a dozen eyes, they seem to sell well too, believe me, I did look into it at one point, I had to, solvency comes at a price!

There's absolutely no doubt about it, a child that dances brings with it an expensive price tag, it will cost you a fortune, but there's a saying;

'Price is what you pay, value is what you get'

I shall elaborate on that with more detail in a later chapter.

And there are tears, yes, of course, lots of tears along the way, and being entirely honest, I admit, totally unabashed, that not all the tears were Danielle's!
Some of those tears were borne from anger, disappointment and frustration, some from the purest combination of joy, happiness and pride, but each tear, like every single penny;
Most definitely worthy of being spent.

As I'll explain as I go along, dancing took a huge amount of my time and now I'm left with a void to fill, a huge crevice of time and unused creativity, and so now, I feel in need of a new challenge, something to replace all those hours spent at the dance studio, at a competition or at home working on or in preparation for something that was going to be needed. My involvement surpassed what might be considered the norm for a dance parent, I was involved extensively, encompassing just about anything and everything.

And now it's gone.

To be fair, it's a void I have created, self-inflicted; it was my choice to make the break from the dance school.

I mean, I enjoyed it; I could have carried on, cutting music, preparing backgrounds for the shows, offering advice, opinion, but for how long, forever? I would have to make the break one day, and that time, opportunity, had seemed to arrive.

Danielle had successfully secured her first professional contract, until that point she was still heavily involved in the school in a teaching capacity, resulting in the need to attend competitions, shows, rehearsals, she needed music for the student's routines, she would make cameo appearances, dancing in the shows.
Her contribution remained extensive, and so naturally, did mine.

But with the arrival of the new contract, and a beckoning career, the time had come to relinquish her role, her time and efforts at the school.

It was a difficult decision to make, I felt like I was walking away from the school, betraying it, taking away all that I contributed, but in reality, that's what happens, within any school, club or organisation, things move on and people move on, to be replaced by the next generation, be that students or parents, and it had come that the sun was ready to set on my time.

I was now faced with a decision, how was I to replace all that time and effort that I had been investing in the school, what new project would await my time and attention, what new project, challenge, could I envisage?

What was I capable of? That was the question.

Well before she was born, I never thought of myself of holding any shred of competency in the basic art of simple parenthood, but I managed, in my own little way. And when Danielle started dance I never thought of myself gaining any level of proficiency as a Dance Dad, but it happened, I never imagined it would, wouldn't have expected that I could, but I did!

So, on that basis, I guess it's feasible that I can take on any new challenge, whatever I might choose, the world is my oyster, he who dares and all that!

Now, I'll be totally honest with you, I'm not too good with heights, and that is a little bit of an understatement, it's a real phobia with me, and it's not actually the height that scares me, it's the thought of falling from it!
More accurately, it's the landing bit that really concerns me; I mean no matter how far you fall, it's the landing bit that does all the damage!

Get me higher than a few steps up a ladder and the dreaded symptoms soon kick in.
My legs go very weak and shaky, I get a sensation in my stomach that spreads into my groin, best described as an intense tingling, now I'll be honest, maybe a bit too honest, but that feeling, in my groins, it isn't all bad, and I suspect, if I got that sensation when on 'terra firma', I might even enjoy it. I offer you an apol-

ogy, for that was probably a little too much information.

I develop an unsettling, loss of balance, coupled with dizziness, and the most unusual, unnatural, urge to fall, yes, ironic I know, looking down from a height and I feel like I need to fall.

Now studies suggest an effective cure for acrophobia, the fear of heights, is a procedure known as, Exposure Therapy, let me explain, some nutter in a white lab coat has suggested, to cure a fear, my fear, I just need exposing to it over a long period, whereby I will then get used to it, and the phobia will cease to be.

So to sum up, take me, along with my death wish, to the top of an incredibly high ladder, with a healthy combination of my weak, shaking legs, my loss of balance and dizziness, a distracting, verging on orgasmic, tingling in my groins, and my unnatural urge to throw myself off the top.

And in the unlikely event that I manage to cheat what seems like certain death, if I don't actually fall, if I should somehow miraculously survive this feat of pure stupidity, I'm cured!

Thanks, but no thanks!

So no, it seems I'm not a real advocate of the Exposure Therapy idea, I don't feel like it would work for me, in much the same way that, had I a fear of being shot in the head, I would welcome an audience with a firing squad

So, being Acrophobic, that rules out most of the fun, exciting possibilities, I guess, so don't expect to glance up to the skies and find me paragliding over a town near you any time soon!

And, being realistic, having just hit the big 5-0, it's probably best I refrain from anything too physically demanding or strenuous, I mean, it's not the thought of running a marathon that puts me off, it's the open heart surgery following it that I would consider to be, a little inconvenient.

So, in my wisdom, after due consideration and much deliberation, I've decided, why not tell my story, share my experiences, re-live them, and write a book.

I mean how hard can it be, surely not as hard as fitting the ribbons to pointe shoes, if you've ever had to do it, you'll entirely understand, if you haven't, I presume you are probably one of those normal people, the ones that wander through life oblivious to the joys of perforated fingertips.

Those needles don't half tickle a bit when they penetrate the sensitive tips of your fingers, and being a novice, at best, seamstress, it was the only way to find out if I was in the right place with the needle,
Actually, I wonder if there is a male version of seamstress, I don't seem to be portraying myself in an altogether very masculine way.

Thank you google, apparently Seamster is a viable option or even tailor; although, in hindsight, I'm not too sure the image of me measuring someone's inside leg is the best way to promote my male prowess.

In truth, I do actually lack male prowess, I lay no claims to being a 'proper man's man'
I have never adopted the laddish, macho, bravado role.

I fail to conform to many of the pre-requisites of true manhood, cars, for example, what self-respecting man doesn't like, understand and know everything there is to know about cars.

If you ever find yourself with the need, a requirement, to point out a car to me, for whatever reason, don't trouble yourself with small details like make and model, even less so nicknames of them.
The colour, that's the crucial information I'm going to need.

A BMW you say, a beamer, no, not a clue, ah the blue one over there, yeah, I see it!

Now can I stop you there, In fact, you don't need to go to the effort of even the colour, I can tell you before you even point the vehicle out, I have no interest whatsoever, in the information you intend to bestow upon me regarding the car, I don't care how fast it can go from 0 to 60, how many horsepistons it has, or the size of that 'bad boy' exhaust.

I have a car, and when I need to go somewhere, I open the door, climb in, drive to my destination, climb out, close the door, and that is the end of our relationship, we keep it simple.

Now real men, they will spend an entire weekend cleaning, waxing, caressing their pride and joy, standing back and survey-ing its metallic beauty, glowing with pride, admiration.
Their wives, lucky with the fact, that the car doesn't fit up the staircase; otherwise, it would be the she, that spent the night, sleeping on the drive, the car in bed, tucked up beside its true love.

Real men will happily tinker with the engine, changing oil, top-ping up water. Me; I'm much more likely to be found under the influence than under the bonnet of a car.

Danielle always says that I must have a faulty chromosome, that I'm actually very maternal in many of my ways.

I have little urge to spend a Friday night out with 'the lads', or to waste a Sunday afternoon, with snooker, darts and a few 'swift ones', at the club, discussing at length the intricacies and finer point of the barmaids chest.

For me that time, is better spent, at home, in the company of my family. I have no need to be surrounded by a large group of friends; I have all I want, all I need, within my little family.

Everybody's different, there's no right or wrong way, and we are all unique in that respect.

Me, I look outside some days and think;

"It's a bit too *'peopley'* out there for me today"

I'm content in my own company, and it's not that I'm lacking in social skills, I'm just not particularly keen on seeking out opportunities to use them.

It's a bi-product of my occupation, an Emergency Medical Technician for the Ambulance Service; it leads to a condition known as *'Patient Fatigue'*, hour after hour spent listening to patients, their ailments, and everything else they have the uncontrollable urge to share with you.

It leads to a want, a need, for on those days off, to not have to listen, to just sit, quietly, cutting a little music, watching a little mind-numbingly mundane TV, and just spending a little time with the family.

Anyway the book, well, more importantly, the writing of it;

Can I do it, can I write it, surely, probably, possibly, maybe, fair enough I have no previous experience or training, aside from an average secondary school education, where I somehow managed to blag a GCE in English Language, and very little else.

Quite ironically, over the years I have developed a love of the English Language, and its use, taking words, the right words, and taking the challenge of putting them in order, the right order to invoke a smile, induce interest, prompt a reaction.

That given, it sounds like a logical challenge, but on the other hand, that solitary GCE qualification, would that prove enough, I mean I only got a lowly Grade C, not exactly what you'd consider to be a worthy accomplishment, one destined to get a classroom named after me.

And not only that, I was born with a congenital disorder, one that would impact heavily on my school years and education.
I was born at the end of August, now anyone else with the same affliction will understand the enormity of being;

'Youngest in the Year'

You're in the same school year as students almost a year older in real terms, a fellow student born in the first week of September will to all intent, be a year older than you in actual age, yet they will still be in the same class as you.
You might think I'm placing a little too much emphasis on this, but trust me people, it matters, a lot, whilst some of my peers would be tackling the finer points of quantum physics.
I was sat at my desk colouring in, not even managing to stay in the lines very well.
And it was crayons; I wasn't even entrusted with pencils!
Too sharp they said, I'd have taken an eye out!

So admittedly, I don't really on the face of it, have the necessary background, credentials or experience to take undertake this mighty of challenges, but with that said, and in all fairness, the only experience I had of dance prior to becoming a Dance Dad was ogling the dancers in the Christmas panto once a year, and I soon picked that up.

As for panto, well I'll let you into a little trade secret here, the jokes, silliness and slapstick comedy, that's for the kids, it's what keeps them entertained for the four hour drag of a journey that is panto.
For the mums it's the glamorous costumes, and the warming 'happy ever after' ending.
And for the dads, it's the dancers! Shouts of *"He's behind you"*
Greeted with thoughts of;

"Well, he isn't, but he wishes he was!!"

Now I apologise to any other dads out there, that I've just implicated with that tiny revelation, it is with deep regret and much sorrow, that and you may now find yourself banned from attending any more pantos.
Or maybe not, you might actually have the urge to thank me, after all, I've done you a favour, I mean, be honest, you've seen one panto, you've seen them all!
"Oh no you haven't!!
I hear you all shout.

So, despite my inexperience, and the minor fact that I'm totally under qualified, what are the chances that I'll actually even manage this new assignment that I will succeed in stringing enough words, the right words, together well enough to hold your attention.
If you're reading this, then I guess I must have made a decent enough start, let's see if you're still there at the end!

Oh well, enough deliberation, I'll just give it a go and see what happens, got my piece of paper and my crayon ready, let's do this!

Now don't think I did this all on my own, this Dance Dad business can be pretty tough going at times and I was very lucky to be blessed with the most perfect of sidekicks, my wing man so to speak, well to be more accurate, my wing woman.

My wife, as she prefers to be referred to in public, or Pam to go by her real name, or Pamela if she's been naughty, actually being totally honest, when she's being naughty she has another name I use.
But that's a digression too far.

Aside from Danielle we also have a younger son, Ben, who has a malevolence towards dance that;

*Only the little brother of a dancing sister can ever
truly comprehend or understand.'*

It's borne from being dragged to dance competitions and shows on a far to regular basis, which to him, would become places where time stood still, a land where minutes lasted for hours, and hours lasted for days.

To give you an insight into how bad it was, he once spent a whole week at a Festival one day!

The number of times at a show I would feel his elbow jab into my side, accompanied by the familiar whisper of;

"How many dances are there left now until the end?"

"Ben, this is the first one, so basically, all of them!" I replied, acknowledging that on this occasion, it was going to be a particularly long night.......for the both of us!

As the night wore on it brought with it many more elbow nudges, followed by the same repetitive question;

"How many dances are there left now until the end?"

"Only three more now Ben, it won't be long" my voice now struggling to hide the obvious exasperation in its tone.

"Dad, how many are there left now?" it was a nudge too far, the nudge that broke the camel's back.

"Jesus Ben! It's the same bloody dance as when you last asked!"

Now, I can't be totally sure, guarantee for certain, that everyone in the theatre heard me, I suspect that there may have been a couple of the grandmas, located towards the back of the balcony, with low battery on their hearing aids, that maybe didn't pick up every single word, but aside from them, yeah, I think pretty much everyone else did.

So, we took the decision, following that debacle, to grant him immunity, a pardon, and not insist on his presence any longer, unless he chose to, of which to date, there have only been the two occasions, the first occasion I will save for a later chapter, and it wasn't even to see Danielle in the show, but as I say, all will be revealed as we go along.

The second occasion being Danielle's first professional performance, Ben knew how much it would mean to her for him to be there, and he stepped up to the plate, he volunteered his attendance, because he wanted to support her in her big moment, and that one act, that one gesture.
Well, I guess that's something that;

'Only the little brother of a dancing sister can ever
truly comprehend or understand.'

And that's how my role as Dance Dad started really, with Pam staying at home to look after Ben whilst myself and Danielle would be off to rehearsals or a competition, it was a sacrifice that she made, and a big one at that, it's can't be easy to know your daughter is dancing and you can't be there, the number of weekends she must have spent, pacing the living room floor, watching the clock with fingers crossed, awaiting, with baited breath, a text message or a phone call bringing good news.

I am so appreciative of the sacrifice that she made, it allowed me to experience those special moments and I will be eternally grateful for that.

On the subject of sacrifice, the life of a dancer brings it in copious amounts, of which Danielle, understandably, had to make many of during her formative years, but it has a ripple effect, like when you throw a stone into a pond, and those ripples of sacrifice spread to affect the whole family.
But luckily, she was blessed, not just in having a Dance Dad, but

in having a dedicated, strong family unit that understood, that supported, we all missed out on things to accommodate those sacrifices, but we did it as a family.

One such sacrifice, prevented us from having a 'normal' evening meal time together, which is, of course, considered a highly important event within most families, a time to reflect on our days, discuss important things together.
But, with Danielle often going straight to the dance studio from school, it was never feasible.

So our, 'family time', always came later in the evening, and it was time that was protected, it would be a time to do something together, be that talk, watch TV or even play a game.

Monopoly, a firm favourite in every household, the foundation of all things good about family time, everyone will have their own Monopoly moments, memories, traditions.

Ours was the game within the game, the plan, that, along with Ben, would ultimately bring the game to an end, with Pam throwing her cards and money across the table, declaring;

"Right, that's it, I'm not playing"

She always started a game completely aware of this intention, it was never a secret, and we would happily gloat about our impending success before a single roll of the dice.

She would fully intend on not rising to any offered bait, stay resolute and strong in the face of torment, but we knew, we all did, even Pam, that ultimately she would bite.

If you poke any animal long enough with a stick, eventually it will react, and some games required more effort, poking a little harder with the stick, but ultimately we would succeed, and the result, always, would be her cards flying across the table. And that would bring an end to proceedings.

I mean, is a game of Monopoly even a game of Monopoly, if it doesn't result in someone's cards flying around the room.

Danielle would have enjoyed the game but become bored by that stage, I would be ready to sit and relax with a glass of wine, and Ben, well he would end up as winner, he always did, that's just how it was.
And that is our Monopoly story, tradition.

Now, just because I mentioned about the wine, I don't want to give you the impression I'm an alcohfrolic or anything.

I allow myself, one, just one glass of red wine, just before I go to bed.
It's just that some nights, I go to bed about eight times.

Another sacrifice is time, when you commit to dance or to any other recreation or hobby I guess, it will consume so much of your time, and when fully committed it can devour a full week-end in the blink of an eye, but it's a choice, there are only 24 hours in a day (unless you're Ben at a show, then there's about eighty!)
But you decide, you choose exactly how you spend them, and together, as a family, dance is what we chose.

So, there you have it, a little introduction to my story and my family,
Now grab those pointe shoes, get your hair in a bun,
And remember no nail polish, definitely no nail polish,

And come join me on my Dance Dad journey.

CHAPTER 2 – THE LITTLE ACORN

'You might never know a man's vulnerable place until you see him with his daughter, because with her, he seems capable of more human emotions than he will ever share with anybody else'

Its 3 am, I'm tired, exhausted, disheartened. Sleep seems but a distant memory, it's three days now since we came home from the hospital with our new-born child, our daughter, our little princess. Three days with little rest and no respite from the constant crying.

I'm downstairs, preparing a bottle, it is formula milk, the first one, a last desperate attempt, emotions are raw, palpable, with an air of despondency filling the room, my mood low. I feel out of my depth, ill-prepared, lacking.

I stare, aimlessly, out from the window; it's a cold, damp morning, bleak, dreary, matching my current mood as I stand on the brink of despair.

The bottle now ready, I head upstairs, my weary legs finding every step of the stairs a mountainous effort.

Approaching the bedroom, the unrelenting crying becoming louder, on entering I see Pam, tired, her expression mirroring my desperation.

Reaching out, I take Danielle into my arms, sit down, offering her the bottle, and suddenly the room is overtaken with a quiet peacefulness, a tranquil calmness, broken only by the sound of her suckling greedily on the bottle.

Looking down to her, staring into those eyes, I see her calming, relaxing, comforted.

Instantly, I feel all those negative emotions drain from within me, replaced, with an almost euphoric sense, a feeling that all is good again.

Your child needed you, something wasn't right, it was causing her distress, and that distress is transferred directly to you, only it's transferred tenfold, and now you've helped her, comforted her, it tips your emotions on their head.

I realised then, right there and then, sitting on the edge of that bed, with her in my arms, yes, this was hard, harder than I could have ever imagined, and true I was totally unprepared for just how hard, but in reality, you can't be, nothing, absolutely nothing, can prepare you adequately, for this immense challenge, this huge undertaking, that is, the journey into parenthood.

In those moments, I could feel a strong resolve building, I could see it in Pam's eyes too, a realisation forming that yes, we were up to this challenge, undoubtedly it would be difficult, demanding, testing that resolve to its limit, but we could do it, I could do it, and I knew at that very moment, that with this little lady.

I was in that vulnerable place, where I would, indeed, be capable of more human emotion than I had ever shared with anybody else.

Admittedly that experience, those emotions, realisations, thoughts, they would not be unique to us, it is something we share with most other first-time, new parents, overwhelmed by those first few days, those initial steps into the world of parenthood.

Reminiscing, looking back, to that most fateful of nights, I recall how I had glanced down to Pam; lay on that bed, with legs help wide, exposed, leaving very little in the way of dignity, seemingly so vulnerable, anxious, and filled with more than a little apprehension.

Understandable, given the enormity of the circumstances, whilst this experience, without question, could be considered to be the most natural of acts, I sensed just how daunting it must seem to her.

Staring up at me, her eyes, flooded with a plethora of mixed emotions, visibly flustered, with hair that was soaked, messy, tangled, beads of sweat dripping from her brow, running down her reddening cheeks.

Her face displaying a fiery determination, through teeth gritted, groans escaped her pursed lips, groans that seemed to grow from deep within her very being, likened to that of a lions roar, echoing around the room like a clap of thunder.

Those moments, when she was overtaken, her body engulfed by those familiar, ever-increasing waves, those sensations; that would result in her eyes rolling back into her head, the likes of which, men will never know, apparently.

A barrage of, what I can best describe as, unadulterated expletives, coupled with a scream, an ear-piercing scream, a scream borne from the truest combination of pure pain and impending joy.

I felt her reaching out at me, her hand gripping the top of my arm, her fingernails biting into the softness of my flesh, causing my face to adopt a slight wince, my mouth forming to allow a little gasp of pain.

She sensed it, turning to face me, very much in the same way, that the young girl in the film, The Exorcist, had done ,when she rotated her head 360 degrees, Pam had even managed to take on the same facial expression too, her eyes speaking loudly to me;

'Don't you dare, don't you even think about making a sound!'

I felt that she was becoming a bit unreasonable at this point, yet it didn't quite feel like the right time to broach the subject, I felt I should leave it until all this was over and done, until she had calmed down a little.

And eventually, finally, with one last push, one last scream, and many, many more expletives, some of which I'm sure I was hearing for the very first time ever.

There it was, over!

Pam lay there, spent, exhausted, her chest still rising fast, catching her breath.

"Ian, I think I'll need stitches after this" I nodded in solemn agreement.

And there it was, that most eventful of nights, that most special time, the moment, when Danielle was conceived!

Nine months later, we were to find ourselves up at the Maternity Unit at the hospital, with Pam in the latter stages of labour.

Now, I'm not going divulge details around that personal, private event, I mean, there's some things that you shouldn't talk about in public!

Now in all seriousness, I do have to say, I have nothing but total admiration for Pam, my own mum, and indeed, all you mothers out there, what you endure, both physically and mentally during the pregnancy and labour, it leaves me in awe of you all. For nine months you allow your body to become a host, a safe haven for that life to grow within you, culminating in that day when you gift your child to the rest of the world.

Being honest, for those nine months, I don't think I fully engaged, Pam would suggest things like leaning towards her tummy and talking to the baby, but it felt strange, funny.
She'd shout me from the bath, when the baby was kicking; I would hurtle upstairs, clearing the steps three at a time, only to arrive at the exact moment that the kicking stopped. To my mind, it would all feel a lot more real once the baby was born.

I can remember, Pam suffering from really bad episodes of snoring during the latter stages of pregnancy, it's just one of those many side effects associated with pregnancy, hormones causing the mucus membranes in the nose to swell.

The snoring would wake me, I would get frustrated, unable to get back to sleep.
On one particular occasion, to the extent, that I de-camped from our bed, to go and seek refuge and sleep on the sofa.
Now there's a lesson to be learnt here; a long duvet, darkness and stairs are not a healthy combination.

As I lay at the bottom of those stairs, tangled in that duvet, sleep deprived (yes people, I realise now, I didn't yet understand, the true meaning of that phrase) and I remember thinking;

"I'll be glad when this is all over, when the baby's
born, and life can get back to normal"
Normal? Back to normal Ian?
There isn't going to be a 'back to normal' pal, ever!

Life changes, it truly does, but in a good way, it changes for the better.

I had assumed, that once the baby was born, I would have a gentle introduction to my role, that whilst at the hospital, Pam would be in charge, have total control, and I would wait until we brought the baby home, where I could be suitably trained up, in the confines and privacy of our own home.

I was wrong!

Within seconds of the birth, the midwife asked me to sit down, and proceeded to then hand me our child.

During the pregnancy, we had decided not to be informed as to the sex of the baby, it only mattered that we were having one, seemingly indifferent to thoughts of a whether it would be a boy or a girl. Using the popular cliché, 'it doesn't matter, as long as it's healthy, as long as it has ten fingers and ten toes'

Not too sure where this obsession about ten fingers and toes actually originates from, I'm sure that are many more pre-requisites to a healthy new-born than just the number of fingers and toes.

So, as I say, I wasn't bothered, boy, girl, whatever, bring it on! Or so I thought, but deep down, sub-consciously, I assume that I wanted my first-born to be my little princess. I base that on my reaction once we finally found out.

All the clues pointed towards the fact that we were having a boy, I say clues, I think old wives tails is probably a little more exact, scientifically proven theories such as;

> 'Your skin is relatively spot-free during pregnancy if it's a boy!'
> 'If you crave savoury food, it's a boy, sweet then it's a girl!'
> 'The bumps all out front, must be a boy!'

So, given that Pam, with her naturally soft, pimple free, smooth skin, a craving for steak puddings, and a bump that arrived places ten minutes before she did, it was almost guaranteed, odds-on we were having a boy, those concrete facts strengthened further by the midwives comments that night, saying that *'baby was being awkward'* followed with *'probably a boy this'*
It was only with that final push, and with the declaration of that midwife;
"He's coming, here he is....oh! ....Here SHE is!

And with those words, those simple few words, in fact, more specifically, that one word, she, here *'she'* is. That was the moment; my eyes began to well up, my bottom lip started quivering, my began heart racing, and a rush of excitement was flooding through me. *She!*

As I sat there, being passed my little princess for the very first time, it didn't feel strange, or uncomfortable at all, I looked down at her, so tiny, so delicate, it felt like I had known her all my life, it seemed as though there was already a bond, now I know that makes little sense, but that was exactly how it felt.

I took in the moment, savouring it, I wanted to take note of everything, remember this moment with a vivid accuracy, a perfect recollection, so as I sat there, with my new-found best friend lay in my arms, I glanced around the room, and thought, quite poetically, you might say;

"What the bloody hell has happened in here!"

The vision before me was a scene of total carnage, there were blood soaked towels strewn across the floor, discarded medical equipment, tissue rolls soaked from the mopping up of, well, put simply, bodily fluids, most of which I never even knew existed. It did not make for a pretty sight!

They were going to have to burn this room down, re-build it, start again with a fresh one; no way can you expect someone to clean this lot up.

Take a minute here, and think, the next time you're having a bad day, when it feels like the whole world is against you, just realise, in a maternity department somewhere, there is a cleaner walking into a room resembling a butchers workshop during Armageddon, thinking;

*"Soon have this little mess cleared up, will have
it spick and span in no time!"*

Once Pam and Danielle were settled on the ward, I went home, I was tired but happy, excited, I felt strong, secure, stable. I was a man, a father! I walked in to our bedroom, to find Pam's pyjamas, left untidily, thrown across the bed, as she had quickly changed to go to the hospital.

"Strong and stable Ian?"
"No, you weren't, were you? Not in the slightest!"
"You started sobbing like a little girl who'd just lost her dolly!"

Yes, it's true, I did, and to be honest, I spent much of that day, either, having a cry, on the verge of having a cry, or having just had one.

I was making phone calls, giving people the good news....ten fingers, ten toes!

I would be fine until they asked what name we had chosen, I would get to Dan, and then my voice would started wavering, my lip going, the *'ielle'* bit, sounding very broken, it's probably safe to say, even now, I cry with consummate ease, in comparison to the time prior to becoming a father.

I think being a parent instils that ability within you somehow.
After visiting hours that night, it was destined that I would go out with a few of the lads from work,

'to wet the baby's head'

I say destined, because the true fact is, that was the last thing I actually wanted to do, I just wanted to go home, sit quietly and reflect, look forward to tomorrow when we would be bringing Danielle home. I wanted to get an early night and a good sleep ready for the exciting day ahead. But it was, as I was constantly being informed, tradition!

And so, as strong, and stable as ever (has a bit of a ring to it that, would make a nice little phrase that, to use in the build up to an election maybe, it's perfect....just had a text from a woman called Theresa, saying I couldn't be more wrong)

I went out that night, just to a couple of local bars, and I wet the baby's head, against my better judgement, and when the relief of last orders sounded, I made my way to where I wanted to be, home.

Since then I have broken with many *'traditions'* opting instead to do what I want, and what I deem best for my family, at times causing annoyance with people, people that don't grasp my take on it. I just don't see the point in doing something you'd rather not, in the name of it being a *'tradition'*, or, *'it's what people have always done'*, well maybe so, but what if they didn't really want to, what if they are doing it for that sole reason of tradition, we'll never stop this madness if someone doesn't take a stand, so I've taken it, feel free to join me anytime.

And so, Pam and Danielle came home that following day, and as I mentioned in the opening paragraphs of this chapter, it was hard, mainly due, in fact, to Danielle not engaging particularly well, in the art of breast-feeding, she just wasn't having any of it.

This resulted, unsurprisingly, in her being constantly hungry, culminating in her adopting the role of, offspring to the anti-Christ, borne from the loins of Lucifer himself.

How on earth, can it be, that something so small, so delicate, so fragile, so beautiful, can make the sound of a wailing banshee that has just stepped onto a plug with nothing on their feet!
And keep it going for hour upon hour.

It was on the advice of the midwives and health visitor, that we should persevere with breast-feeding, and when I say advice, I actually mean threats, at times abusive, brutal threats, that's how it felt anyway. The mere suggestion of bottle feeding met with a cold, steely stare, eyes showing little other than disdain, scorn and contempt, suggesting you'd not simply enquired about something that you thought might benefit your child, instead feeling like they had just walked in to find you dangling your daughter by her feet, over the bannister rail.

I can only assume, that following the fall of Hitler's regime at the end of the second World War, a splinter group, a breakaway faction formed, going underground, for, however long it takes to complete a degree in midwifery I guess, only to return, and rise stronger than ever, intent on global domination, on ensuring every single baby was breast-fed, seeking out the weak and vulnerable, preying on parents to the new-born.

Following a heart to heart between myself and Pam, we decided that when the health visitor came the following day, we would inform her of our decision to bottle feed, and we would stand by that decision, we would fight, we would oppose that totalitarian regime, and we would do what we, as parents, thought best for their child.

Now at this juncture, I should inform you that, generally I am a very laid back character, avoiding confrontation at all costs, taking the easy route, walking away from trouble, but on this occasion, the weight of responsibility that lay across my shoulders, the responsibility that I had to my daughter, it instilled a little fight within me. I spent that night preparing for battle, formulating a strategy, pre-empting her comments, rehearsing the answers in my head, it played on my mind, but it wasn't going to keep me awake all night, that was Danielle's job!

And so the knock at the door arrived, I came face to face with my foe, we greeted each other in the hallway, I with a friendly welcoming smile, her with an obligatory Nazi salute, and we proceeded in to join Pam and Danielle in the living-room, where we spoke about our decision, and in all fairness, she was very nice, understanding, there was no war of words, no arguing.

I wondered if I had, in fact, misjudged those highly skilled healthcare professionals doing their amazing jobs, and that my opinion had become clouded, tainted by the delirium, tiredness that had engulfed me, either way, Danielle started on bottles, and it was as though they had swapped her with another baby, she was so much happier, much more content, which meant, so were we.

We had made our first, of many, big decisions in her life, and we'd got this one right.

In hindsight, Danielle's appetite was always going to cause a problem, you see, she has a major problem regarding her appetite, I'm not sure of the actual medical term or condition, but put simply, her appetite is....massive, verging on the insatiable at times, even now, to this day.

Many times, I will look across to Pam or Ben, with an exasperated;

> "It needs feeding....it's getting angry, it needs food,
> for god's sake just feed it, quickly!"

I suspect, many of you readers, maybe even both of you, yes I've got high hopes for the success of this book, will assume that I have used a little poetic license that for effect....trust me, I haven't;

> 'A mother scorned'...............'A wounded dog'

They don't seem quite the danger, once you've encountered;

> 'A hungry Danielle'

Now, in those early times, I used to take Danielle for regular walks in the pram, now I say walks, they could be more likened to expeditions really, I was a firm advocate of the health benefits of pure, simple, fresh air, and with us out of the way, Pam was free to tackle the million and one jobs that she would be doing that day, hey, I just remembered, I left my shorts on the floor at the side of the bed this morning, make than a million and two jobs.

And so it transpired, those walks would end up, a minimum of at least two hours taking in miles in distance.

It's weird really, but I used to talk to Danielle a lot during those long walks, in my head, seems strange doesn't it, I mean, lay there asleep and oblivious, just weeks, months old, she offered little in terms of response, no feedback, no advice, no laughing at the funny bits.
She just lay there, unassuming, seemingly unaware of my madness.

But here's the thing, it didn't feel like madness at all, it didn't feel weird or strange, it felt natural, the norm. A special bond allows for little things like that. We had, very soon, created the most special of bonds, and it was a bond that would get stronger every single day, even during those, supposedly, awkward troublesome teens, when I expected I would probably lose her to adolescence for a while, but no, she allowed me to share that time too, I remember one of her friends watching us interact at the studio, her words, with an air of disbelief;

"You two are so cute! ....Do you never fall out, have words, argue?"

Danielle's reply, causing me to smile;

"Nah, never....he wouldn't dare, he's far too scared of me"
There's an expression;

'Many a true word, spoken in jest'

As you have probably guessed, I could and happily would, wax lyrically about the bond we share, for the rest of this chapter, at least, but I won't, it will become tiresome and boring, what's that you say, too late Ian!

I will round off with the words from the most beautiful of songs, one that Danielle and I, with that special bond, can fully relate to.

It is an acoustic duet, a soft country ballad, written magically by Glen Ballard and Alan Silvestri, and performed with perfection by father and daughter, Billy Rae and Miley Cyrus.

First heard, in the 2009 film, Hannah Montana: The Movie.

It charts the progression and transition from childhood to adulthood and the support of a loving father.

And for any of you out there, wondering, interested,....yes, my bottom lip is wavering right now, and a teardrop has just landed on the keyboard.

Enjoy, these beautiful lyrics;

You tuck me in, turn out the light,
Kept me safe and sound at night,
Little girls, depend on things like that.

Brushed my teeth and combed my hair,
Had to drive me everywhere,
You were always there, when I look back.

And when I couldn't sleep at night, scared
things wouldn't turn out right,
You would hold my hand and sing to me.

Caterpillar in the tree,
How you wonder, who you'll be,

Can't go far, but you can always dream.
Wish you may and wish you might,
Don't you worry, hold on tight.
I promise you, there will come a day,
Butterfly, fly away.

◆ ◆ ◆

Now if told you I would sing Danielle a bedtime song every night, you would reasonably assume it to be that one, but by its release in 2009, Danielle was already ten, and her bedtime song was established in the preceding years, at a time when Danielle was very young, impressionable, trusting.

That song was 'Coward of the County'.

Now I can almost hear your disbelief of that fact, yes I agree, it was a bad choice, it wasn't suitable, it wasn't relevant or appropriate, in any way, shape or form, the reason for that choice, well, basically, I knew all the words and I liked putting on a deep, husky, slurred, Country and Western accent.

Now I know what you're thinking, why didn't you pick a nice, happy, jolly Country and Western song, ...have you listened to Country music? There aren't any happy go lucky ones, someone's either died, dying or missing, or cheated on, drunk, and lonely, that's it folks, your options.

But even so, yes, I agree, it was the strangest of choices.

For those of you that don't know the song, I will offer a little insight;

Basically it's a tale of a young man, a lovely young man, devoted and loyal to his loving wife. He has a bit of a run in with a family, a group of brothers.

I say a run-in, it was more the fact that these brothers gang-raped his wife, leading him to attack them all in the pub down the road, resulting in him being condemned to prison.

Yes, just perfect children's bedtime matter, what little four year old girl doesn't want to close her eyes, hear the bedroom shutting, leaving her alone with just those graphic images filling her head? I don't know why, or maybe I do now, but Danielle had the biggest collection of teddies and dolls with her every night, at bedtime, in hindsight, maybe it was in an effort to provide a bit of normality, sensibility, safety to the proceedings.

She would have a ritual, it would include our special handshake, it would take up to twenty minutes just for that alone, and then I had to stand there, whilst she had kissed every single one of those toys in my presence. Danielle had become, very early in life, the master of delaying tactics, adding on slowly but surely over time, to be honest, I had to match her ingenuity somehow, but how?

"Everyone considered him the coward of the county; he never stood one single time to prove the county wrong"

"Nite Dad"

"Nite Squidz"

Squidz, that's what I call her, we all do it don't we, a kind of pet name, nickname, a term of endearment, affection, a name who's meaning and origin, makes sense to only the two of you.

The journey to that final nickname, Squidz, begins with the popular expression;

'you can't kid a kidder'

So initially, she became known as *'Kidder'*.

That developed into *'Kiderooni'*, then later to *'Squiderooni'*, shortened finally to *'Squidz'*, or her stage nickname, *'The Squid-ster'*.

On one occasion when she was ill, I coined, quite cleverly I think, the expression;

'I'd rather have a fiver'
Now, you've all just adopted that same blank expression
that Danielle did, so here's the explanation;
'I'd rather have a fiver than a sick squidz' (six quids)

I always feel jokes don't work particularly well, if you have to explain them.

On the subject of Danielle being ill, it's something she doesn't do very well, she is blessed with many skills, but being ill is not one of them, the slightest blemish on her skin leading to a frantic search of Dr. Google, revealing the probability of some form of Melanoma skin cancer.

A bit of a tummy upset leading to the assumption that she's developed a twisted bowel obstruction. She becomes increasingly frustrated with my apparent lack of concern on the subjects, especially with the suggestion that we should set up a fundraising and awareness campaign;

The Danielle Corson Foundation for Sore Throats!

Now, back to that bedtime song, as bad as it was I think everyone should be allowed one little *'faux pas'*.

"But there wasn't just the one, was there Ian, tell
them about that other musical mishap!"

Well, firstly, I should explain, I am big fan of the musical, The Rocky Horror Picture Show, it's a cult classic, newlyweds Brad and Janet, stumbling across the mansion owned by Dr Frank-N-Furter, a bi-sexual, transvestite scientist, played with such aplomb in the film, by Tim Curry.

It's a show we have been to see on many occasions, it's one of my favourites, now as some of you may already be aware, there is this thing, whereby the audience dress up and attend the show as characters, on one occasion, we had tickets with my brother and his wife, and collectively we agreed to go in character costume.

For the strangest of reasons, I had selected the main character, yes the bi-sexual transvestite, I ordered my costume on-line, and soon after I came home from work one Friday afternoon to find the postman had delivered the package. I went upstairs to try it on.

I'll be honest with you all here, it wasn't a success, for the costume comprised solely of a black Basque, black stocking and suspenders. Now, imagine, actually please don't, don't even begin to picture it, you won't sleep for weeks.

I'm alone in the house, my bedroom no less, kitted out in this costume, with bits hanging out where there shouldn't be, and things not hanging out where you'd expect them to be, it really was not a pretty sight!

Thoughts suddenly filling my head, what if I suffer a medical emergency, what if I'm suddenly left incapacitated, that was going to be a treat for the ambulance crew;

> *"Of course sir, a show, yes, for the audience, yes*
> *I fully understand, now if I just pop this blanket*
> *over your stockings, we'll be on our way"*

Add to that, the cold realisation that today is Friday, yes Friday, the day the window cleaner turns up, and I'm suddenly running aimlessly around the house, in a vain effort to find a safe haven, but let me tell you something I realised very quickly, in a house, during the day, whatever room you go in, it has windows, and the curtains inevitably, will be open.

In a mad panic, I attempt to undress quickly, get out of this costume, I'm hit with a further revelation, a basque stocking and suspenders are difficult enough to get into in the first place, but getting out of them, near impossible!

Not helped by the fact, that my hands have started shaking, I'm sweating, and the clammy material is now, seemingly welded to my skin.

I fall backwards onto the bed, flailing around pointlessly, then it hits me, logic, it always takes a while for it to arrive in these situations, but better late than never!

The curtains!

Just shut the curtains, and with a leap from the bed, I grasp them and close them, quickly, now lay in a heap on the floor, I look at myself, one stocking around my ankle, the other down to my knee, ripped, and I decide, there and then, I will go to the show, and I shall go in costume, but not this one, definitely not this one!

In the end, I went as the character Riff Raff, the costume.... trousers, shirt, jacket, what's not to like!

Now I know what you're thinking, a bi-sexual, transvestite scientist, this doesn't sound like the kind of film you'd encourage a five year old to watch, would you.

"Well Ian, would you, did you?"

Ok, guilty as charged m'lord, but in my defence, it boasts some amazing music, catchy up-beat numbers, come on you've all danced along to The Time Warp;

"It's just a jump to the left, and then a step to the riiiiight, put your hands on your hips, and bring your knees in tiiiiiiiiime"

See, I told you it was catchy.

My theory was, that the inappropriate content, well she would be too young to understand it, and it would just go over her head.

Now, as I say, those songs are very catchy, they get stuck in your head, even a little five year old girls head, and there must be many times, and many places, that a little girl could choose, to suddenly burst out in song, one of those Rocky Horror classics.

I didn't foresee, that my little five year old girl would choose, the classroom, at school, yes, in class and giving her very own little rendition of;

"Tu tu tu tu touch me, I wanna get diiiirrrty"

Luckily, for me, it was Pam charged with picking Danielle up from school that day, all you parents know the drill, that moment, waiting in the yard, spotting the teacher looking around, searching for a particular parent.

"Mrs Corson, can I have a word please?"

Now nothing grabs the attention of the other parents in the

yard like those words, the yard falls silent, and they walk past, slowly, deliberately, as close as they dare get, hoping to grasp every little detail of that child's misdemeanour, to regurgitate the story the following morning, to all the other parents.

In all fairness, the teacher took it with good humour, indeed, herself a Rocky Horror connoisseur, she actually found it funny, she said it wasn't so much the words she was singing that were the issue, more the facial expression and gyrating hips!

Kind of puts Coward of the County into perspective doesn't it.

As I said, it was Pam that had to deal with that situation. Now I think it only fair I give you a little introduction, background to my partner in crime, my wife.

We've been together since we were just 18, recently celebrating our Silver Wedding Anniversary together, she has blessed me with two wonderful children, and a more loving wife I could not ask for, like any marriage that lasts the course, there have been bumps along the way, naturally, and it is those bumps that make you stronger, more robust.

When we work together, we form a formidable team, both bringing different things to the table that, that combined result in success.

To my detriment, if I'm honest, I have to admit, I'm not the most lovey-dovey of types, romantic gestures not really my thing, well not in the traditional sense, and you know me and traditions, so I show my love in other ways, there are many different ways to say, I love you, for example;

Following a twelve hour night shift, with four hours sleep, and another shift waiting that night, greeting her on her return from work;

" The kids have had their tea, I made it after I picked them up from school, don't worry about the washing-up, it's done, so sit down, put your feet up and I'll bring your tea in for you in a minute"

All done, so that on her return home from work, she wouldn't have to do it all herself.

To my mind, the worth of that is more than of three little words, it says the same thing, but in a gesture, it has substance, a meaning, and an act that not only says. I love you, it shows it to.

Now when I say acts, gestures and the like, I don't mean holding hands on a walk, definitely not, or worse even, walking arm in arm, that has to be the most unnatural of things. I watch in dismay, a couple, arms around each other, failing miserably in an effort to step in synch, looking more like they are out training, practising, looking ahead to the upcoming World Championships for the three-legged race event!

So to sum up, she probably has a lot to put up with, in respect to me, but put up with me she does, and I'm very grateful that she does.

I remember back, twenty-five years ago, standing at the front of the church alongside my best man, my brother Jamie. I glanced over my shoulder, my eyes met with a vision of true beauty; I saw her standing there, in the aisle, silky hair flowing down her back, her eyes bright, sparkling. Her make-up was done to perfection, highlighting those soft cheeks bones, those bright red lips, how I wanted to just run down the aisle and kiss those soft, warm, sensual lips.

But the wedding march music began to play, it was time.

She sat down, taking her seat with the other guests, and Pam appeared at the top of the aisle.

Now, of course, I was jesting there, and that kind of sums up our relationship, in many ways she is my Ernie Wise, my Tommy Cannon, my Ronnie Corbett.

All the best double acts have a 'fall guy', one to which the other will use to gain a laugh, a funny moment, but don't be fooled, I do it with total respect for her, she is a wonderful wife and amazing mother, she is selfless when it comes to us, she will do anything and everything for us, and I'm filled with nothing but total love, admiration and respect for her.

We to, are one of life's greatest double-acts.

Now, back to our little Acorn, Fridays took on a great significance in those early years, I would finish work at lunch-time on that day, and we would have the full afternoon together, we always did something, be it swimming, an afternoon at the seaside, whatever it was, it became special, because we were doing it together, *'daddy-daughter'* time, it's precious, money can't buy those moments.

So much so, that when she was old enough, and started school, those Fridays, those afternoons, they became an abyss, I felt like I had been deprived of my right arm, it left such a massive void that took me a while to recover from.

Fridays took on a new meaning, we made the night special, to replace it, not just daddy-daughter time, family time, as we would all sit down together, with popcorn, crisps and chocolate and share a movie, it became known as;

'Friday Night, Film Night!'

It's the little things that hold the sweetest memories.

Now, on one particular *Friday Night, Film Night*, we had chosen Disney's Lion King, I'd never seen it, but it seemed to be popular, and Danielle related to it because of the holiday we had not long returned from it.

It was on that holiday that Danielle had her first foray, her first outing onto the stage; the hotel would put on nightly shows, on this particular evening that show was to be The Lion King.

Earlier in the day we were approached by the Entertainments staff, asking if they could use Danielle in the show that night, she agreed, and as instructed, I took Danielle backstage early, to have her make-up applied and costume fitted, I have to say, the cast were amazing with her, making a real fuss of her backstage.

She was to play Simba, the lion cub, on stage at the beginning, for that iconic scene where Rafiki, the monkey, holds Simba in outstretched arms, announcing his arrival into the world.

Now, the show was in Spanish, so in truth, I had little idea what was actually happening, but I what I did know, was that Danielle was back on stage, being lifted again, in the same way at the end of the show, leading me to a misinterpretation of facts, that would prove highly significant on watching the movie.

Just a little side note, the show, in Spanish, I liked that, why shouldn't it be, we were in Spain after all, too often, in my opinion, people expect everything to be English, even when abroad on holiday, and I like it when those expectations are not always pampered to.

So, fast forward to *'Friday Night, Lion King Film Night'*, we sat there enjoying, as a family, a good old family favourite, all totally oblivious to the impending upturn in events, that would lead, to the untimely and sad demise of Simba's father Mufasa, Danielle was distraught, sobbing uncontrollably, broken-hearted, tears streaming down her face.

Luckily, I'd seen the show, I put a comforting, confident arm around her;

> *"Don't get upset sweetheart, there's no need to cry, you see, he's not really dead, he's there at the end, trust me, I promise "*

I mean, I'd seen it with my own eyes, the end of the show, Mufasa, standing there, alive and well as Rafiki, held aloft another young lion cub....

Yes, I know, I know, but it was in Spanish!

Of course I realise now, that the character I thought was Mufasa, was indeed a grown up Simba, but it was in Spanish, and if you're going to use the exact same actor for both parts, it's going to lead to a certain level of confusion.

There's a bit, later in the film, that puts beyond doubt, that dispels any hopes, any thoughts regarding Mufasa's mortality, it is an upsetting moment for any young child, but a child who's dad, the one man in which she would always be able to trust, rely on, when he promises, well that just compounds the upset, it becomes even more distressing. In all honesty, in hindsight, it was probably just good training in preparation for watching Marley and Me!

I made a decision very early on in the journey of parenthood, with the knowledge, that children grow up very quickly, I didn't want to miss a thing, with either of them, that I didn't fall into the common trap, of;

'I can't wait until they are, such and such and age and are...'.

Or

'I wish they were, this age again, I miss....'

I took every day, in the present, enjoying, savouring, all they had to offer, and I'm so pleased I did, we both committed all our time to them, devoted every minute to their wants and needs, and there is no regret, we could probably count on one hand, the number of nights out we have had, just as a couple, always choosing instead, something than was inclusive of them.

And, to my mind, why not, I mean, if you're going to have kids, why wouldn't you want to spend all your time with them. I recall taking them to the swimming baths one time, all there, as a family, having fun in the water.

My eye was caught by a dad, sat at the side of the pool, as his wife played in the water with his three children, now I accept, there are a million possible reasons as to why he wasn't in the water with them, and I could have no idea what that reason was, but the more I watched him, I noticed he just sat, reading a book, only taking a moment to look up to watch, when prompted by a *"dad, watch this"* shout from one of his children.

It bothered me, more than it should have, I found it quite sad, but in truth I know nothing about that man, his family, or his reasoning, so I should refrain from judging too harshly.

I should, but I won't;

"You got kids man, they are right in front of you, they are having fun, splashing around, for gods sake, watch them, share those moments, for quickly, very quickly those moments will be gone, and they will have grown up"

I say, that having children was the best thing I have ever done, and it truly is.

I was lucky, very lucky, to have the most perfect of role models, my own dad, yes, I too was a little acorn all those years ago.

I always think that my dad was ahead of his time, in a generation fixated with;

'The woman stays at home, cooks, cleans, and brings up the children'

No my dad was far in advance of that generation, ahead of his time, he sent my mum out to work, the cooking and cleaning, well she'd have to do that after work!

I'm joking obviously, she did in fact work, as did my dad, he worked nights, so pretty much most of the household duties were shared, he did his bit, yes it might have resulted in an abundance of Crispy Pancakes for tea, the most popular after school offering I can recall, but we were fed, and we were well looked after.

Together they were amazing parents, we didn't get everything we wanted, but we got everything we needed, and they too would deprive themselves for our benefit must be where I got it from, a tradition so to speak, yeah yeah, well, some traditions are worth keeping going.

I am forever indebted to all they have, and continue to do, they had three of us, and we've all turned out pretty well, so they must have got something right!

CHAPTER 3 – I AM THE MUSIC MAN

"I AM THE MUSIC MAN"

"I come from down your way!"
"What can you play?"

"Nothing, absolutely nothing!"

"Not a single, solitary, tuneful note on any piece of musical equipment whatsoever!"

Blessed at birth with tone deafness, an instinctively natural ability to make the most simple musical instrument sound like two cats fighting over a fog horn, (ultimately entrusted with, well demoted to, more specifically, the triangle in music class, I lost the metal stick and had to try and make a noise hitting it with my finger, the result, in my humble opinion, as dull as the lesson) and with a voice best suited to a career within the silent movie industry.

I make claim to no musicality prowess whatsoever, not a single ounce of capability or aptitude.

However, that said, should you have the need or requirement, for a song or a piece of music for a dance routine, then I truly am your man, I am indeed the music man!

TheMusicIan! (Yes, I know, that's a very clever play on words, Music and Ian, my game/my name, adjoined to create The Musician), to be fair I'm not totally sure there was a need to explain that, I should give you a little more credit, it is quite self-explanatory really, however, I cannot claim the credit for the name itself, as it was actually Danielle who thought of it in the first place.

So simple, yet so very clever, and that pretty much sums up my music making ability, simple yet, at times, very clever!
How did it happen?
Well, they do say that;

> *'Necessity is the mother of all invention'*

And that kind of explains how.

Ironically, in my latter school days, the very fleeting moments that I gave my career aspirations even the slightest thought, and believe me, those occasions were very rare, and evidently not altogether realistic, I suspected I would have to make the difficult decision between becoming a professional footballer or a radio DJ, high ambitions indeed for a boy who didn't even regularly make the school football team or attend any music lessons!

But it's strange when I look back now and think of the DJ route, I seemingly had then, unknowingly, or more accurately, unwittingly, a desire to work with music, an untapped route for my creativity, little did I know back then, that when I finally started growing up, in my 40s I mean, (and I mean started, in terms of fully growing up, I'm yet to become the finished article), I would use that hidden talent to achieve the self-revered title of *TheMusicIan!*

In the end I settled for an engineering apprenticeship, altogether more attainable, but ultimately so much less rewarding.

❖ ❖ ❖

I'm a strong believer that girls mature much, much quicker than boys in their formative years, and consequently, are much better prepared for life beyond school.

In her early teenage years, ask a girl her plans for the future, and she will outline her total strategy, in detail, with a specific timetable of events, starting with the GCSE passes she intends to gain, to allow her to attend a definitive college for specific courses, gaining the appropriate A level qualifications to attend the university of her choice.

Graduating with a specific degree to enable her to gain an internship with a particular company, incorporating a gap year spent hiking around the Himalayas with a purple unicorn backpack.

Promotion to the role she has worked so hard to attain, meeting and then married to the man of her dreams at 26, taking a break from her job to raise her 2 wonderful children (one of each) before returning to a successful career, until reaching her early 50s, when she will retire early to look after her even more wonderful grandchildren (two of each).

Ask a teenage boy his plans for the future, and....

"Erm, dunno, having egg and chips for tea, not sure after that!"

I was Mr Egg and Chips....with ketchup on the top, literally, I lacked ambition, aspiration and gave little or no thought to life

beyond school, to be fair, I don't think it helped that I was the youngest in my year, did I mention that already?
See, it really does bother me!

And in all fairness, things have advanced, schools have progressed in terms of the opportunities they can offer, there is so much more choice available, and if a student has a particular skill or ingenuity, it can be accommodated.

In truth, English and Maths will forever be the mainstay of our education system, and rightly so, it's like ballet, whilst not every student likes it, and be honest, most don't, it's important, it's needed, yes it can be boring and arduous at times, whether it's mastering a Grand Jete or solving a Differential Equation it's not fun, it's challenging and demanding, but it remains imperative to everything else.

But also now, fortunately, in this current era, there exists alternative windows of opportunity, for example, Danielle, she was lucky enough to be able to study Dance at school, as a subject within the curriculum, culminating in a recognised qualification.

My choices;

"Woodwork or Metalwork! Take your pick!"

So, necessity the mother of all invention.
Well in the early days of attending dance competitions, we were a small dance school, reliant on the help, as most dance schools

are, of the parents, and at one of those early competitions each individual school was responsible for playing their own music for their dances, time for '*TheMusicIan*' to step up, or '*TheJibberingNervousWreck*' as I was known back then!

I kid you not, as simple as just sitting there and pressing play on a CD player seemingly is, it actually really isn't, when you look up and see a 7 year old in starting position awaiting the music, watching their chest rising and falling quickly, their heart visibly pounding, fear etched on their innocent face, hands trying to remain still but noticeably shaking.

It's a time that requires calmness and confidence, someone to just simply press play, but I suddenly notice I'm shaking to, the room is filled with silence, anticipation, expectation, I can feel my heart pounding so hard I'm convinced the entire room can actually hear it, adrenaline is pumping through my whole body, the finger I need to press play with doesn't feel like my own, I fear I can't control it, I think it's gone numb now, I can't feel it, I can't press play, swallowing is proving difficult, my mouth has become so very dry, maybe the beads of sweat forming on my brow might drop onto my lips and hydrate me, panic is starting to take over.

I can sense the eyes of the audience focused solely on me, filled with expectation, a muffled cough breaking the silence, yet making me jump, distracting me, distracting me from what though?

"The button!"

"Press the bloody button Ian!"

I'm overthinking this, calm down and press play, the dancer

glances across at me, her eyes pleading for music, her expression begging me, pleading with me to pull my finger from my arse and use it to press the bloody button!

Come on Ian, just calm down, take a deep breath and press play, what could possibly go wrong?

Everything, that's what could go wrong, absolutely everything!

What if it's the wrong song?

What if I press the wrong button?

Is the cd function even set, what if I press play and the radio blurs out?

> "Stop it Ian, you're overthinking this, just press
> play! For the love of God, just press it!"

A leap of faith and there, it's done, I pressed it, I only bloody did it!

I nailed it!

The music plays, it's the right music, I sit back in the chair, smug, overwhelmed by my sense of achievement, nothing to it!

Play needed pressing and I was the man that did it!

I'd like to say that I sat there and enjoyed, savoured the most beautiful dance routine, in truth it was all a bit of a blur, it didn't even register, I was consumed with relief, distracted by my now calming nerves, and I decided there and then I was never doing this ever again, it wasn't worth all the stress.

I would hand the baton to someone else.

But you know those hangover moments, that feeling in the pit of your stomach that spreads when you're suddenly hit with the realisation, the memory of an event from the night before, well it was just like that.

I looked down at the running order.

> "Shit!"

"We're up next too!"
"And this time it's Danielle!"

It's all just got very serious, very serious indeed, the stakes have just doubled and I'm trapped in this chair, stranded, I look over to where the other parents are sitting, in the hope that I can get someone's attention, get someone, anyone, to come and relieve me of my duties, now call me cynical, but I failed to catch any-one's attention, not through a lack of trying, but because those other parents were clever, they were wise, they had just seen the hellish ride that I had just endured and there wasn't a chance they were going to allow even the slightest eye contact.

I was on my own, and, oh good, this dance has just finished, a little round of applause, the obligatory curtsy, and here we go, here's Danielle, the look of absolute fear across her face suggests she saw my previous episode, I looked down, staring at my ad-versary, my antagonist, my foe, *'the button'*, and with a steely de-termination, I whispered to myself;

"Come on Ian, you can do this!"

And I did, and in truth, it was never quite as bad after that, I think I was a bit guilty of overthinking the whole thing, I mean, it's just pressing play surely.

But if you've ever had to do it, you'll understand, and if you haven't you won't, and if the most nerve wrecking thing you've ever done is to take a penalty in a World Cup Final, well you won't understand either!

Following that baptism of fire, I actually grew to enjoy the role as *'play'* presser, and became known from then as the music man, admittedly the tiniest of claims to fame, but one I enjoyed.

However, the more I sat there and listened, not just to our own, but to every schools music offerings I became aware that for all the effort and practice that had gone into the choreography, the routine, the performance and the dance moves, there was something not quite right, and it was the music!

It was, a lot of the time, overlooked, underestimated, for me; the most beautiful routine would be spoiled when the song was overtaken by a background hissing, a miss-timed cut or a sudden, abrupt ending.

I realised that it was an important part of any performance, be it an exam, a competition or a show performance, for a dancer to give their best to any dance they need to have a connection to the music, if that music is flawed, so will the connection, and no matter how technically good a dance is danced, the performance will suffer, and when that happens it's a shame, because it has failed not because of the choreography that the teacher has spent hours creating and teaching, not because of the dancer who has spent hours learning and cleaning that dance but because of the most simple thing, the music!

I looked at what I deemed important, firstly the volume, I'd sit through a competition or show, one minute struggling to hear the music of one routine, only to be followed by music blaring out, shaking the rafters.

So, step 1; set all songs to the same volume, simples!

The big problems dance schools suffer from with respect to the music is the length of the song, let's say, for arguments sake, that the average duration of a song is three and a half minutes.

Unfortunately for exams and competitions there are pre-determined time limits, age and section related, so a routine might be, for example two minutes long, now the key is to translate that three and a half minute song into those required two minutes, enter those abrupt endings, random fades that leave a dancer looking lost at the end of the routine, and harsh cuts where music is roughly joined together.

Now, breaking it down simply, the majority of songs have a beginning, a middle and an end, therefore the new, two minute version needs to reflect and incorporate, where possible, those three stages, there is an alternate option available with music intended for show routines.

Simply keep the song the original length.

No No No No No!

It rarely, if indeed ever, works, it's so difficult to keep the same dance fresh and interesting for that long, it can become boring and repetitive, especially given that certain sections of dances will get constantly repeated to accommodate the longevity of the song.

So there lies step 2, smooth transitions when cutting with definite endings.

I presume I'm coming across now, especially to any dance teachers out there, that I'm being over critical, self-righteous and very picky, that dance is about dance, not the music, *(that's it Ian, there's a top plan, dance teachers, probably your biggest target audience for this book, carry on, go alienate them, annoy them, patronise them, see how that plays out in terms of sales!)* but I've sat through hundreds and hundreds of routines that tell me different, it's horses for courses, I can't choreograph a single move, I can't teach one, but I can provide music that facilitates those skills best, and pass it to the people best placed to use those skills, those wonderful dance teachers. *(Good efforts Ian, win them back, get them back on side, suck up to them)*

A routine is a tapestry woven in the beginning by a concept, coat that with the right music, good music, well cut, and you have the perfect platform, a foundation to craft the perfect choreography and perform the most amazing of routines.

How many times, at a competition, have you heard the adjudicator comment that there was very little between the dancers, the routines or the technique, that she selected a winner just out of personal preference, the routine she enjoyed the most, I wonder what part the music played in that process.

So, that's how it all started, I wanted our dance school to have the best music, to hopefully lead on to having the best routines, so I set out to learn how to achieve those two steps, I spent time learning how to use music editing software. And as the old adage says, practice makes perfect, it was not uncommon to spend hours on something only to dismiss it, throw it away and start again, but I soon realised how much I actually enjoyed it and the sense of achievement I gained from a finished piece.

I recall during a visit from one of Danielle's friends, Helen Handshaker, of course that's not her real name, I mean that would be silly, a name like that has to be made up….. Helen!

Ok, jesting aside, yes it was the Handshaker part that was made up, it came about from my very first meeting with her, it was at the theatre following the college dance show, as she walked over to me, laden with bags full of costumes. Danielle introduced us to each other, I held out a helping hand, an offer to relive her of her bags, to do the gentlemanly thing and help, she responded by taking my outstretched hand and giving it a very swift yet very firm handshake saying;

Very pleased to meet you"

I should explain that Helen is probably the funniest female I have ever had the pleasure of meeting, her humour is contagious, it's very laddish in its nature and delivery at times, and she can make me laugh with such ease, so I guess our introduction was always destined to contain a funny moment.

Anyway, back to the visit, Helen was upstairs with Danielle in her bedroom, probably discussing the finer points and complexities of Love Island or Geordie Shore.

Myself, I was downstairs, cutting and mixing a version of *Rag n Bone Man's 'Human',* it was taking time, I was overlaying sound effects, playing with different versions of the song, for over two hours I was playing with it, and apparently you could hear it upstairs, now I'm not totally sure why it took two hours for what happened to happen, but it did, finally, after two hours, Helen turned to Danielle and said,

"Jeez, you're dad really likes this song doesn't he!"

She genuinely thought I was sat there just continually listening to it, over and over, for listening's sake!

But that's the thing, I considered it the norm to spend so long getting something right, it mattered not how long it took, it just mattered that it was right, I took much pride and self-satisfaction when I would play a cut piece to someone, Danielle the usual victim, and they could not guess where it had been cut, yet it was the next stage that proved most satisfying, creating a mix of numerous songs into one track, playing with cuts and timing to get that perfect transition, when one song blends seamlessly into another.

It was at that stage when I realised that the ability to achieve multi song versions opened up even more creative possibilities, I could overlay sound effects, voices, I could alter the speed or tempo of sections, add special effects, echo's and the like, it opened up so many possibilities.

I started thinking about the pre-music stage, I could think about ideas for a dance routine, think of a scenario, a concept, something I thought would be effective, something different, as I say I can't choreograph a single dance move but I can, kind of have a vision in my head of a routine and then create the music to fit that.

The difficult part is to translate that concept and vision to the choreographer, to successfully transfer the idea relied heavily on their perception and how receptive they would be, it always worked best with Danielle, she would intuitively grasp what I was thinking, and teamed with her amazing ability to choreograph, the result were some fantastic routines that were immensely successful and just as important, very enjoyable to watch.

It would seem to make perfect sense, a natural progression, begin with a concept, choose a piece of music best suited to it, and then, only then, begin the choreography, it sounds simple, yet you'd be surprised just how often I will be asked to cut some music with the instruction;

"I've already choreographed up to one minute twenty"

(There he goes again, upsetting the dance teachers, he'll be lucky if anyone other than his mum ends up reading this book!)

Aside from the difficulty it can cause in respect to blending the beginning, middle and end sections, it limits the opportunities, to create something special, something different, something interesting, and surely that's what those dance teachers really want; a routine that stands out against a backdrop of the norm, something that sparks an adjudicator's interest, I mean be fair to her, she's been sat there for hours, at times having to watch the most mundane of routines, ones the like of which, she has watched many times before, her concentration is less on the routine, and more on faking that interested look, or on her attempts to remain focused.

So give her that something different, grab her attention, capture her imagination, grasp her focus, and see how it is reflected in those marks.

I'm assuming, following this book, *TheMusicIan* will be inundated from dance schools and teachers, with requests, appeals, demands. I can hear them now;

"Please don't write any more books"

"Take your book, your music, your opinions, and stick them where the sun don't shine"

I sincerely apologise if I come across as a little self-important with regards to the music, but to me, it is important, I genuinely love it. I am passionate in my words, because it means a lot to me.

It's funny, and I'm sure all you dance teachers will say the same, all that time and effort invested in music, it comes at a cost, and that is, it then becomes impossible to just enjoy and listen to music, be that on the radio or wherever, without wondering about it's potential as a routine.

I would become distracted by it, even just watching television was affected, the background song to a scene, or an advert, often using a different obscure version of the track, and it would plant a seed.

The number of times the family would groan, as I apologetically disrupted their viewing.

Jumping up to rewind the TV, standing there, playing it into *Shazam* on my phone, searching frantically for its origin.

However, it's like anything, else, it's a numbers game, for every ten ideas, there might be a couple of good ideas or concepts, and even they might fail, maybe I wouldn't explain the vision well enough, or it would get misinterpreted by the choreographer or the dancers, and when it fails, because they can be quite radical ideas they can fail on a big scale, but when they work, they succeed on an equally proportional level, and when that happens, the results are amazing and the feeling unbelievable!

I remember at the time that *Little Mix* were in the charts with '*Secret Love Song*', I had listened to the words and thought how extensive their meaning could be, many different people would interpret those words in their own way.

There's many reasons why a relationship would need to be kept secret, race, sexuality, religion, personal situations, family expectations, I immediately found it interesting as a routine, I went looking and found a slow version of the song, one to match the dance style.

At that time Danielle was looking for a new duet, I'd already had an idea but really liked the thought of using this piece as an idea instead.

Using the duo as a lesbian couple who kept their relationship a secret due to social pressures and fear of acceptance, it totally matched the song in my opinion, so I cut a version and suggested it to Danielle, who initially wasn't too keen.

Whilst she loved the idea, she questioned whether it would be judged too radically and be unpopular with some people, her sentiment ironically mirroring the concept and song, when she turned up to rehearsals and told her dance partner Polly the two ideas, they discussed them before Polly bravely suggested to Danielle

"Let's do it!" "Let's do the secret love song!"

I failed to take Danielle's concern to seriously as I believed, maybe a little naively, that homophobia was thankfully on the decline, and that in this current era, people were much more accepting.

But sadly, at the routines first outing at a competition, Danielle's fears proved justified, it bombed, it crashed, it absolutely died, and it wasn't because of the dancing or the performance, they had dance it beautifully, and technically very well.

They got the lowest mark ever, now given there was nothing lacking in the performance, it was presumably because of its content, it amazed me to learn that homophobia was alive and kicking, surprised even more that it was in the performing arts environment, which had proved so ground breaking and receptive over history.

I found it quite sad really, but it gave us an increased drive, not to give up on it, a heightened endeavour to make it work, to make it accepted.

Its next outing was at a big National competition, Danielle and Polly getting into character for the whole day, for that entire day, they were a couple, in love, unashamed of any reactions.

It's a lesson to every dancer out there, believe and feel your character, engage with the song, consume the words and the sentiment, they did that in their performance, it was amazing and they won the whole competition with that one routine, it was well deserved, and one of those times when the vision in my head transferred to the dance floor and the feeling was something special.

And their prize, a free place and stay at a competition at Disneyland Paris the following year.

So with my appetite for finding songs and cutting and mixing them growing, I decided to expand my services, I had learnt to create music for Danielle's dance school, Ktz Dance, and they had allowed me to hone my skills, as I said not all my ideas were good ones, whilst I had blessed them with some great ideas and music, I had also lumbered them with some bad ones.

Ironically, one such failure had its sole outing at the very competition that Danielle and Polly had won, it was a version of the *Boomtown Rats* single, '*I Don't Like Mondays*', for those of you too young to know, it was a song written by lead singer Bob Geldof following the 1979 Cleveland Elementary School Shooting, carried out by a 16 year old girl, Brenda Spencer, when asked why she had committed the act, she replied simply, I don't like Mondays!

Now I know what you're thinking;

"Radical? Radical??"

"Your ideas aren't radical, they're verging on the insane!"

"A school shooting, very appropriate!"

"Should go down right a treat, that should!"

Bear with me, and I will prove you right, very right indeed.

So, I found a version by a group named *G4*, a British male vocal troupe who had finished second in the first ever series of X Factor, I think in truth, that was their highest point, I'll be honest, I'd never even heard of them until I stumbled across this version of the song.

It was delivered with a slight operatic undertone that suited the mood and content of the song, I recommend you go and find it and have a listen.

"Stick with me lads; I'll soon have you back in the charts!"

Anyway, I took the song, I cut it, I added sound effects, newsreel commentaries, but it didn't stop there, there were gunshots, children screaming, sirens, all you come to expect from a young kids dance competition really!

It's funny, but as I'm writing this now, reading it back, what was I thinking?

Surprisingly, inexplicably, against all the odds, it failed to impress the judges, the audience, or even the dancers, Danielle confided in me later, that is was actually embarrassing having to actually dance it, she hated every second of it.

So there you have it, my most momentous failure.

That said, very much in the way that a parent will defend unconditionally, the actions, or wrong doing of their child, how they will seek excuses, a reasoning for those actions. I still think there is potential in the idea, I think the biggest failure was in my attempts to explain the vision, the concept in my head, the finished routine far from what I had initially conceived.

A part of me would like to revisit it, try again, take it from the depths of despair and like a phoenix from the flames, watch it rise from the ashes, and finally gain success.

So, if there's any dance schools out there, looking for a challenge, wanting to stand out, and trust me you'll stand out for sure, Danielle said there was a lot of pointing going on, not just during the performance, but for much time after, so come on, be brave, let's do it!

It's funny, I can almost hear Danielle screaming now;

"Nooooooooo!"

So, in summary, it's like anything, it's a learning curve, and I was thankful to Ktz for allowing me practice at their expense, but the time had come where I felt proficient enough to offer my services to other schools, to expand my base, it soon became evident that there was a real need for those services, it seemed lots of dance teachers agreed with my opinion on the importance of well-cut music and the difficulty in obtaining it.

I loved it at first, but soon it became a burden, I didn't have enough spare time to keep up with all of the requests and it became less fun and much more of a chore, so I took the decision to step back from it.

But one particular dance school got my attention, I liked their ideas, and they had some amazing dancers , one of which I was lucky enough to watch via video link, performing at the *Dance World Cup Finals* in Barcelona, a young boy, an amazing talent, a product of that fantastic Dance School, and I smiled, a little self-satisfied smile, as I watched him dance on that biggest of stages, to my music, yes mine, ok I wasn't singing, or playing any instruments, but I had cut it, so I was claiming it, my music!

It was a pleasure to do their music, which I still do even today, affectionately known as Miss J, Jackie from *Roberts Morgan School of Dance*, became a friend and I learnt so much more about dances from cutting her music, and I was touched that when Danielle got her first professional contract on a UK production tour, Miss J turned up to watch one of the shows.

I really appreciated that sentiment, it meant a lot to not just me, but Danielle too, it was her big break, her first professional work, and she liked it when people made the effort to go and watch her, so....

Thank You Miss J x

❖ ❖ ❖

Now aside from my music commitments within Ktz Dance, I had also adopted the role of Video Man, it was a role that began almost entirely by accident in truth, initially just filming Danielle's dances for nothing other than posterity, but as I'm sure you've guessed by now, when I get involved with something it does have a tendency to snowball, pretty soon I was filming other dancers routines too, at a competition at the famous Tower Ballroom in Blackpool, each school was allowed a single person from the school to record the routines, and of course, it was always going to be me.

Although it had risks attached, it wasn't as daunting a prospect as the initial music man encounters, it seemed simpler, or maybe I was just getting used to things a bit better.

I then found myself an associated project, I would spend time at the studio, in lessons, taking photos, recording videos, gaining enough material to construct and produce a promotional video, you know the kind of thing, a minute long collage advertising all the school had to offer.

Well ten minutes later, yes ten minutes, I think I got a little carried away, but, in all fairness it made excellent viewing, to the extent that, Katie confided in me, that on watching it for the first time, she had cried, tears of happiness, her school was growing, and seeing it on the screen, highlighting by how much, it proved emotional for her.

As I said, filming Danielle's routines were a way of capturing a memory, to look back on in time, but as she advanced, there became another reason, she wanted me to film them so she could study them, as soon as we would return home from a performance she would request the video, and she would sit there intently, watching, dissecting, analysing, it proved a useful tool, you can spot things, identify and highlight errors that are so easily missed or overlooked, in real time.

So much so that we started to use the technology in a lot of her group dances.

Towards the end of her time at the school, as part of her teaching role, she formed a 'Street' Team.

I would watch at rehearsals, knowing when something hadn't gone quite right, but unable to specify exactly what it was, my eye picking up on something, but not able to keep up with the speed of it, and so I started filming them, we could watch them back later, it enabled her to spot the error, sometimes watching in slow motion, or frame by frame.

It worked well for positioning, out of time movements, in all fairness it was a little severe, brutal, there became no place to hide, if someone got something wrong, it was there to see, a case of;

'Now I'm not looking for someone to blame, but whose fault was it?'

But that's a good thing, it improves the dancer, and it improves the routine, and it showed.

Some of those dances ended up so clean and impressive.

I ended up with quite a collection of dance videos, and set up a YouTube channel, I would film at competitions and show, then after uploading them I could post the link on the schools social media sites and the students, teachers, parents could enjoy them all over again.

I'm not sure I could lay claim to being a *'tuber'* in all truth, but with over 200 subscribers and fast approaching a quarter of a million views thus far, it's proving quite popular, go take a peek if you like, *ossygobbin68*.

So once I was happy with the music and video side of things I looked for a new challenge, and as was, always the case, one soon appeared, the school had reached its 10th Anniversary and plans were afoot for a special Show in celebration of the achievement.

Katie had asked me if I thought a stage backdrop/projector screen would work
I immediately embraced the idea, and set about working on it.

It was time consuming, frustrating at times, but I started sourcing the most suitable background videos to match the dances, initially the idea was to basically just have a picture on the screen, but videos or collages were proving more impressive.

Imagine the most beautifully danced lyrical routine, now imagine behind, covering the whole back of the stage area;
> *Fluffy white clods, floating slowly across the back*
> *The moonlight, shining in the dark sky*
> *Stars, twinkling brightly, flickering*

It was, as you can imagine, extremely effective.

To see that Anniversary Show, the celebration of ten years of the school, in a packed theatre with professional lighting, video backdrop, great music, amazing costumes, all topped with wonderful dance routines, many of which Danielle had choreographed and taught, it was quite emotive.

To think back to the schools humble beginnings, where early shows would be performed in a school hall, it highlighted to me just how far the School has progressed, how far Danielle had progressed and how far I had too, that night I felt so much pride, for the school and all involved, for Danielle and for lil ole me too!

When I look back on my involvement during those ten years, it brings realisation to just how much I contributed, the vast time and effort that I had invested, and whilst I probably didn't get everything just right all of the time, I like to think I made a difference, I played my part in the school, and its students progression.

And that thought, well it instils a heart-warming sense, a feeling of achievement, deep within in me.

◆ ◆ ◆

Being so heavily involved granted me presence at the show theatre rehearsals on the nights and day preceding the performance.

I found my happy place, I adored the environment, the stage, the lighting rigs, the whole setting, I loved being so heavily involved, I gained so much pleasure from preparing for those shows and, to this day, I miss it a lot.

I can't help but think that if the young Master Egg and Chips had known about all this back then, things would have turned out a little differently, whilst I'm certainly no performer, a career backstage, in the background, that would have suited me just fine.

*"I am the music man; I come
from down your way"*

CHAPTER 4 – DANCE DADS ARMY

'The only way to make sense out of change is to plunge into it, move with it, and join the dance' Alan Watts

'DANCE DADS ARMY'

Remember back in the prologue, when I mentioned that Ben only volunteered his presence at a show on two occasions, you didn't know there was going to be a test did you?

"Just do what I do, either go back and read it again to get the answer, or as I more commonly do, just blag it!"

I'll remind you, it was Danielle's first professional performance and one other, well here's one other.

I'd said earlier that I was in a happy place when backstage at a theatre, well that's not strictly true, backstage, waiting to walk out onto the stage in front of a large audience, well, that's a not so happy place!

The dance school were invited to attend a competition, and it was to be held at the Disneyland Paris Resort, in France.

An amazing opportunity indeed, but alas an expensive one, travel, accommodation and entry fees, they all mount up.

So what do dance schools and parents do at times like this, take it on the chin, say;

"Oh well, never mind, maybe another time"

No, they rally round, they do whatever's needed, they go that extra mile, they will do anything and everything to make those dreams come true, and when I say anything and everything I mean exactly that, been there, done that and actually really do have the t-shirt.

There were the raffles, sponsored events, the normal things you grow to expect from a fundraising operation, and then there were;

'Dancing Dad's'

Yes, that's right, dads dancing, well I say dancing, there's a certain poetic license in the use of those words.

I suspect there is a long forgotten rule in the English language, that forbids the use of those two words together; dads dancing!

I mean throw in a word or two in between and all is good in the world again, dads *'at'* dancing, dads *'watching'* dancing, dads *'paying for'* dancing!

And so it transpired, myself and five other misfortunates, dads from the school, were recruited to form our own little dance troupe, looking back, none of us can actually recall agreeing to our involvement, but more importantly, none of us actually refused, as had other, more sensible dads, and so it just kind of happened.

We would learn, we would practice, we would re-learn, and practice again, and again, it was going to be an uphill struggle, but it was going to be fun, and it would culminate in a fundraising performance at the next show.

A three minute routine, showcasing our newfound talent and skills, and Ben, well, be honest, what self-respecting teenage son doesn't want a front row seat to watch his dad make a complete fool of himself. He sat on his seat at that theatre for six weeks, popcorn in one hand, vodka in the other, waiting, day and night, giggling in excited anticipation, never before had he experienced this level of excitement ahead of a dance show.

So the plan, yes, we had a plan, we were taking this serious, if we were going to do this we had to, granted, we couldn't take ourselves too seriously though, I mean, we were dads and we were dancing, but we planned to give it our best shot, with the show just over six months away, we commenced our journey, undertaking our first rehearsal.

Now don't think we were a close group of friends when we began this mission, in truth, we hardly knew each other, our only common denominator being that, our children attended the same dance school.

You can imagine just how awkward those first few moments in the dance studio felt, and I think all of us were probably a little guilty of this, I most definitely was, secretly hoping that they, the other dads, were all totally rubbish, worse than even me, in all fairness, that was probably an unfair expectation, after all, I knew just how bad I actually was!

We stood there, six individuals destined to become a team, lined up in front of Katie.

I suspect she felt just how Louie Walsh had felt, when Boyzone had first stood before him.

That same feeling, instinctively knowing you're on the verge, the brink of something special, and believe me, all of us, in our own little way, could be deemed 'special'!

Danielle was on the team to, a bonus for me I thought, extra personalised rehearsals at home, will give me an edge that, or maybe not!

At this juncture I should probably introduce you to the team, I thought I should probably change their names, protect their identity, safeguard their reputations, allow them to remain anonymous.

But then I thought, no chance!

Name and shame, that's the way to go!

So here they are ;

Chris, he was the one that I knew least when we started, I'd seen him around but we'd never spoken, I soon realised what I'd been missing out on, I soon learnt how funny he was, his sense of humour just on my wavelength, he made me laugh a lot.

His downside was his attendance record, which at best, would be considered atrocious, in his defence, it wasn't actually his fault, he had a close friend by the name of Jack, and he had a disruptive influence on Chris, we all had full time jobs and personal commitments, and finding a rehearsal time suitable for everyone was difficult.

Friday nights becoming the most common that we could all attend, but Chris used to visit Jack after work on Fridays, and however much Chris genuinely intended to turn up for rehearsals, an hour or so in the company of Jack and that would change, Jack would convince him otherwise and so often it would end with Chris missing from the rehearsal.

It's a credit to him that he actually made it to the end, I only missed one week and I never really grasped the section that the others learnt that week, so for him to miss so much, yet still perform, and perform well.

I take my hat off to him, and his friend Jack Daniels.

Brett, a committed member of the background team at the school, along with his wife Eunice, they would do whatever was needed, whenever it was needed.

It's a pre requisite, for the success of any small school to have parents like these, they rely heavily on them and their unconditional devotion to the cause, and as a bonus they are an all-round lovely family.

Now Brett was a real bundle of energy, nervous, excitable energy to be more exact, he was probably the one who thought he was struggling when he wasn't, he would get visibly frustrated if he couldn't grasp something, but that happened with all of us, we all struggled at times, although it did become a standing joke that whatever foot we would start on, Brett would start on the opposite foot.

Not so much a standing joke, more of a stepping joke really.

Scott, the youngest and probably one of the fittest, he was our 'eye candy' member, the one that would hopefully distract the audience away from watching any of us others, he was also one of the better ones at picking up and remembering the moves, he was our very own Ronan Keating.

Andy B, of similar age to myself, we were the more mature members of the team, in years at least.

However, the immaturity in our sense of humour contradicted

those years, I mean, be honest, put a group of men in such close proximity, throw in a combination of bends, stretches and thrusts, and the jokes pretty much write themselves, at times we laughed so hard we had tears running down our legs!

Andy was also instrumental in the props department, he spent many hours making our *'pièce de résistance'*, a loony tunes logo, that we smashed our heads through, just like in those cartoon titles.

Andy F, his fitness closely matched with his dry, very dry, sense of humour, forever etched in my mind his comment;

> *"I think you'll find, we're doing all the right moves,*
> *just not necessarily in the right order"*

Homage, of course, to that late, great talent that was, Eric Morecambe OBE.

Andy worked hard, he was good, he was the one we looked to for help, when we'd forgotten a couple of the ten moves we'd learnt the previous week, he was our go-to man!

So there you have it, the motley crew of individuals destined to share their *'Andy Warhol'* fifteen minutes of fame, and fifteen minutes it very nearly, almost was.

You know how, whenever you assemble a group, any group, there's always one member who seems determined to ruin it for all the others, one individual intent on bringing the whole plan crashing down, one person, whose sole actions can have a catastrophic, damaging, detrimental effect to the whole operation

Ladies and gentleman I introduce the final member of our team, me!

As I said, we had a plan, it was simple, we'd rehearse, practice, get up on stage, do a quick three minute routine, get off, and disappear off into the sunset and never speak of it again.

Enter *'TheMusicIan'*, now I've spoke at length about the joy of creating concepts and making music, well put simply, I just couldn't leave well enough alone, the three minutes grew, slowly but surely.

The number of rehearsals, at which the lads would be greeted with;

"Ian's had another idea and added some more music"

Now, I can only presume Ian is a bit thick, a bit slow on the uptake, what Ian struggled to comprehend, was that whatever Ian added to the music, Ian had ultimately to go and bloody dance it!

I mean be honest, you're going to do a dance, yet you can't actually dance, you have no previous experience coupled with absolutely no natural rhythm.

There's going to be a big audience, it's going to be captured on film, it's going to find its way to Facebook and YouTube, but luckily, your saving grace, you have total control over the music, more importantly, you have control over its duration, what do you do, keep it simple, even dip under the requested three minute bar.

Well Ian, did you ?

*"No Ian, you didn't did you, you added and added,
you were still adding the week of the show!"*

*"The only thing that stopped you Ian was there
was no more time, you ran out"*

"Well done Ian, good effort, amazing job, it ended

up at 11 minutes, 11 seconds long!"
"Three minutes, that's all we wanted"

But no, as was more accurately articulated by Andy F;
*"We ended up with 11 f****** minutes and 11 f****** seconds!"*

So there we stood, on that dark, cold January evening, assembled in the dance studio, our first lesson, our first foray into life as a dancer, now at this point I have to say, to all you dancers out there, whatever your age, whatever your level, I am in total awe of every single one of you.

Having spent hours over the years, watching lessons, classes and rehearsals, I've seen how you would spend half an hour, to learn and remember up to a minute of a dance, I genuinely do not know how you do it, I am filled with total admiration and respect for you.

Our rehearsals would last for at least an hour, we would learn, intently, with full concentration, around six seconds of the routine, to return the following week with little or no recollection of at least half of that.

This was going to prove a big challenge indeed, fortunately, we had six months, and luckily, it was only going to be three minutes long!

The words that will forever be ingrained in my mind from those rehearsalsl;

"Now, moving on...."
"Woah!, woah!"

DIARY OF A DANCE DAD

"Can I just stop you there, moving on? Moving on?"
"I haven't grasped these 2 seconds yet, moving on!

I kid you not it was so much harder than I ever imagined, I'd spent so much time watching dances, rehearsals, shows, competitions, I considered myself quite the expert, highly qualified in my opinion, I would sit there, casting a professional eye over proceedings, making notes in my head.

Now very often I could be guilty of being quite critical, spotting a mistake, a miss-timed move or I'd be bemoaning the fact that a dancer wasn't using their face, now therein lies, possibly the number one critique of any developing dancer;

"You need to use your face, how hard can it be?"
"Just use your face!"

But now, on this journey, this voyage of discovery, on the crest of this massive learning curve, well, I actually get it, I totally understand!

This entire dancing malarkey, it's so much harder than I ever gave it credit, more difficult than I anticipated.

Under instruction I was learning to move an arm in time with the music, I could even manage both arms if they were to do the same thing, but legs to, at the same time, doing something totally different?

"I'll be honest with you here love, you're expectations
are a little high, too high, my arms will move, my legs

will move, but never the twain together!"
*"And if the expectation is that there will be anything
from this face other than a fixed, blank stare of deep
concentration, determination and focus"*
"Well then, someone's going to be very disappointed!"

As soon as my face starts to move, revealing some half attempt, a mere semblance of expression, my limbs stop, they just cease moving, put music on and my legs can move, my arms can move, my face can show emotion, just not all at the same time;

"So take your pick, which do you want?"

I expected that I had a card up my sleeve, an advantage over the other guys, I had a personal teacher at home, my own private tutor, in hindsight I probably needed one who had a little more patience with me to be honest, or put simply, she just needed a student with a little more ability.
It didn't work well, I recall snapping on one occasion;

"I'm not a dancer; I've never done this before, give me a chance"
Her reply, the tone filled with total exasperation;

*"But dad, this bit isn't even dancing, you're just walking
in time to music"*

And it was, all I had to do, was take a few steps forward, it was walking, how hard could that be, I'd been doing it for years, and unless I'd indulged in one too many glasses of wine, I had pretty much mastered the art.

Only, previously, there had not been any importance placed, on starting with a particular foot, or on taking a step at the right time, in tandem with a specific beat of music.
And that was the point, everything becomes so much more

difficult when you have to do it in time to music, and at exactly the same time as five other people.

I think ironically, our weakness became our strength, the numbers game, being six of us there was a slight chance that at least one of us was doing something at the right time, however the chances of us all doing it together, at the same time, well that resembled the same chances as successfully nailing jelly onto a wall!

And so rehearsals progressed, and in time, confidence began to flourish, and the routine started to take shape, we had props, we had gimmicks and we even had a few moves that would hopefully impress our audience, and as I was constantly reminded we had over eleven minutes of music!

I grew to enjoy our time at the studio, I think we all did, yes it was hard, yes it was demanding, but we became a close group.

There exists, an air of vulnerability, when allowing yourself to 'dance' in front of others. Once on stage, in front of an audience, those moves would be practiced, rehearsed, polished, but in the studio, when attempting a move for the very first time, under the scrutiny of your peers, you can feel, naked, exposed, susceptible to ridicule.

It is testament to how close a team we had become, because when an attempted move went wrong, and believe me it happened, frequently, on many occasions, yes, it was met with ridicule, but in a good, comfortable way, it was banter, the kind of which only works when there is a close bond.

It resulted in much laughing, many jokes, and some very memorable moments, it got to the stage where I would actually be looking forward to rehearsals, and that was all down to the team, yes I was undertaking this crazy mission, yes it was stressful, but I was lucky enough to be doing it alongside these amazing people.

And as is so often the case, it's not the actual event that you're doing that is special, it's the people you're doing it with that makes it so.

◆ ◆ ◆

The couple of weeks preceding the show, rehearsals increased, anticipation was building, all rehearsals were behind closed doors, so nobody had a preview of the routine, no-one had the slightest inkling as to what it would be, but there was a buzz around it, people were looking forward to it.

The plan was, that the show would run as normal, there would be a short intermission to allow all the dancers and backstage helpers to join the audience.

Just what we needed, a bigger audience!

No one wanted to miss this, and being honest, why would they! If I hadn't been so heavily involved, I wouldn't have wanted to miss it either!

On the eve of the show, we had a theatre rehearsal, so for the first time we stood, and we danced on that stage, and at that moment, that exact moment in time, the realisation, the enormity of what we had undertaken hit me like a freight train, what was I thinking?

Dancing? Me? In public?

I looked out across the auditorium, from an unfamiliar vantage point; the stage!

Ahead, rows and rows of empty seating, how I wished it was going to be empty the night after, but alas, I knew it wasn't going to be!

I felt sick to the pit of my stomach, nerves overwhelming me, I'm sure I wasn't alone, as my glance passed over the other lads, I became aware of the loud silence, it was rare when we were together, there was deep contemplation underway here, there was fear, it was raw and it was real.

But, it was soon to pass, the silence was broken with a joke, accompanied by more than a few expletives, and we did what we did best, we laughed, we joked, and we got on with it.

Something else I'd never given much consideration to was how difficult it is to dance in a place other than where you've learnt and practiced: the studio.

It's disorientating in the extreme, it's surprising how many little 'markers' you have, that you're unaware of, a scuff on the floor, highlighting where to stand at a certain point of the routine, a certain brick on the wall, holding much significance, we had mirrors at the studio, here there were none, obviously!

I'd never realised either, that stages are sloped, it makes sense if you think about it, it elevates slightly, people at the back of the stage, making it easier for the audience to see them, it's not something you notice sat in the audience, but standing here, on this stage with a gradient on a par with Ben Nevis and a magnetic pull from the edge of the stage, it was a concern, I had a premonition that on walking to the front of the stage, I wouldn't be able to stop, instead picking up pace, speeding up until I fell head first from the edge, landing on the rows of young children below, admittedly there was little rationale behind these images, but desperate times lead to desperate thoughts!

Added to all that, and this might sound strange, and possibly make no sense at all, I mean the studio and theatre were miles apart, but strangely, and this will prove difficult to explain, probably even more difficult to understand, it felt as though we were facing the wrong way.

Now I don't know if we are programmed, as humans, with an in-built compass or something, a natural ability to sense North, East, South or West, you're just going to have to trust me on this. We were definitely facing the wrong way, we could feel it, and we didn't like it.

Now faced with the unlikely fact, that overnight they were going to rebuild the theatre to face the right way, we were going to have to adapt, but it had unsettled us further, forcing us to hastily arrange an impromptu, last minute rehearsal the following morning, the day of the show.
Panic and blind fear lead to knee jerk decisions like that.

So, the day of the show finally arrived, we spent most of the morning and early afternoon at the studio, last minute prac-tice, rehearsing the routine, facing in a different direction in an attempt to acclimatise to the theatre, yeah I know, a futile at-tempt at best, and generally trying to keep each other calm.

I say calm, it wasn't calm, not at all, not in the slightest, but we were trying our utmost to avoid delirium and hysteria, no easy task given our impending performance.

On arrival at the theatre it all started to feel very real, and more importantly, very imminent.

We watched a lot of the show from the auditorium, but in truth saw very little, our minds elsewhere, distracted, panicking on which particular part of the routine we would forget, or mess up.

I liken it to those moments just before an exam, when you realise you've forgotten just about everything, and try as you may, it feels like you can't remember the slightest shred of information.

We lost Chris for a while, we never actually found out where he had gone, but a gambling man would probably risk a little wager that it was the pub across the road!

And so we stood, at the side of the stage, peeking through the curtain at our waiting audience, you could feel the anticipation out there, the excitement was palpable, there was a buzzing, humming from the audience, a noise I can't really explain, then suddenly;

Silence, a cold, brutal silence, as the auditorium lights dimmed. It was the worse silence I'd ever experienced, it was deafening, yes I know that doesn't make sense, but neither did me standing at the side of that stage, but I was!

We were totally alone backstage, we were afraid, very afraid, and we could sense every single person sat, waiting.

It was my job to pull the cord to open the curtains, and when I got my cue, when the music started, all eleven and a half minutes of it.

"Yes Ian, eleven minutes, you total dick!"

And there it was, the music started, I pulled to open the curtains and at that moment, that very moment in time I was enveloped by total, unadulterated fear, my legs had gone like jelly, they were shaking, they felt numb, walking was going to prove a tad difficult with these bad boys right now, so dancing?

My heart was pounding, I had pains in my chest, my stomach felt like it does on a rollercoaster ride, my hands shaking like never before, I really didn't want to be there, my mouth was dry, I couldn't swallow, I looked across at the lads for support, their faces mirrored mine, it's funny how all the jokes and witty comments dry up just as the shits about to hit the fan!

I had an increasing urge developing, to just stand here and watch, from the side, yeah, good plan, no one will notice, I'll just stay here, no problem Ian, screw the lads, they're on their own now, just save yourself!

"Good luck to them, but it's every man for himself,
women, children and MusicIans first!"

"I'm just going to stand here and watch!"

I have no idea what force took over me, but something did, despite my resolve, my decision to just stand, something was carrying me out onto that stage, some external force, looking at the legs beneath me, deceiving me, betraying me, walking out onto that stage.

I remember looking down at them and thinking, you'd better know what you're doing!

And luckily, they did, and the greeting we got from the audience helped quell the nerves, the room filled with supportive welcoming cheers and clapping, it was a fantastic reception for us and pretty soon we were actually enjoying the experience.

At one point early on, you know Ian, with his Acrophobia, yes that Ian, the one who was prone to stupid ideas in the name of a 'clever concept, that will work well' yes that Ian, well, there was an elevated section of stage, at a guess approximately fifteen feet high, with no barriers.

"So why Ian, why on earth, where you the one to make an entrance on to that bit of staging, dressed in a pink dressing gown, and donning a shower cap and loofah, why Ian, Why?"

In all honesty, I was so pumped full of adrenaline, I didn't care, the level of fear to which I was already exposed could be heightened no more. I guess that nutter in his lab boat had the right idea with his Exposure Therapy theory after all..

I know what you're thinking now, pink dressing gown, shower cap, loofah, are all his ideas this radical and crazy?

Well, yes, guilty as charged, they probably are, I could attempt to explain the theory and reasoning behind the outfit, but it would probably be easier to just show you. Now there's an idea, hands up anyone that wants to watch these dancing dads!

Ok, here you go, as I said earlier, it was always destined to reach the realms of YouTube, so here's your opportunity, enjoy!

https://www.youtube.com/watch?v=_CItrSapTqQ

It feels like this book has now become a little interactive, I can't help but wonder if there's a generation of readers out there, so used to touchscreen technology, that are pressing the link with their finger in expectation of a video appearing, I'm afraid not, you'll just have to type it.

And so, as you have probably just watched, the show progressed, and those eleven minutes, well they actually only felt like three, it passed with such speed, there were good parts that worked well, there were parts that were not so good, that didn't work quite so well, but all in all, and I'm sure you'll agree, it passed relatively trouble free, and by the end, well, we were buzzing, absolutely buzzing with a combination of excitement, relief and spent adrenaline.

The auditorium was rocking with applause, cheering, whistling, flowers were thrown onto the stage, somebody threw a pair of knickers at us, and I suspected it to be my mum, as they took three of the lads down!

But they soon recovered and got up, only slightly battered and bruised.

The feeling, as we stood on that stage at the end, basking in the adulation, savouring the applause, it was something I had never experienced before, I understand now, what drives performers, dancers, actors, comedians, I imagine it can become quite addictive, that craving for applause, adulation, acceptance.

I had that craving, stood there, that night, I wanted to do it again, right there and then, I doubt, physically and mentally I would have actually been able to, but the urge was there, no words can ever begin to describe how it feels to experience that moment, to know how it feels, you would have to do it, go on, I dare you!

As Andy Warhol said, fifteen minutes of fame people, now go

find yours, I can highly recommend it!

Despite vowing never to repeat the experience, a few years later came the schools 10th Anniversary show, now be honest, how could we not!

But this time it was going to be a surprise, no one was to know anything about it until we stepped out onto the stage, it became a closely guarded secret, so much so that one of the lads hadn't realised we were at least able to tell our wives, he turned up at one of the early secret rehearsals saying;

> *"I think I need to tell Pauline about this, she's very suspicious, she wants to know where I keep disappearing to on Friday nights, she thinks I'm up to no good"*

So in an effort to avoid any impending divorce proceeding, the wives were all informed of the plan, aside from them, it was just us lads and our new teacher, our new taskmaster, Danielle, that knew.

Sadly we had lost Chris from the group, he was unable to commit, he had recently become a dad again, and his time and effort was, as you'd expect, needed elsewhere.

And so it came to be, the fab six, became the fab five, if Take That could overcome losing Robbie Williams, then it suggested we could manage without Chris. In all honesty, I was sad he couldn't join us the second time around, he had played an integral part in my enjoyment the first time around, and it has to be said, I missed having him around at rehearsals, although to be fair;

I missed having him around at most of the rehearsals the first time around!

So, under Danielle's leadership, the plan was that we would re-create a popular routine that the street team had performed with success, it had placed, against all expectation at a big competition held at the famous, Winter Gardens Theatre in Blackpool, it was an amazing experience and a wonderful night, and consequently, the routine held fond memories for the school.

So it seemed only natural, that it should be the routine, that we would choose to do. Danielle had choreographed the routine initially, so was well placed to teach it to us.

It soon became evident that, there was going to be the need for a few tweaks here and there, '*TheMusicIan*' finally becoming useful, we slowed sections of the music down, to adapt to our inability to match the speed of the original dancers. We changed a section that, even had we continued rehearsing to this day, we would not have achieved some of those moves, but in the main, it was fundamentally, the same routine, and with Ian having learnt his lesson, it was only three minutes long!

We had to let Katie in on it eventually, surprising her with an impromptu performance at the studio one night when we were fully rehearsed and nailing it, ok, bit of an overstatement that, in all honesty. But it was at a point where it was ready to be shown, she was thrilled, she was excited about the impending Anniversary Show as it was, but that night, we handed her the cherry, to go on the top!

On teaching us the routine, it has to be said, Danielle coped so very well with us, she had us under control, no easy feat for a young girl with five immature men, but she did an amazing job, so much so that myself and the lads had a collection between ourselves, raising enough to surprise her at the end of the show with a card, flowers, and I suspect, a well needed, bottle of vodka.

And so, following the plan, we stood at the side of the stage, again!

But this time, with fewer nerves. Less fear than what was present on the previous, first occasion.

The audience were oblivious to our impending performance, just ten minutes earlier I was sat in that audience, alongside Pam and Ben, whilst they knew about it, my mum and dad, also sat with us had no idea, so much so that I had to fake receiving a text from Danielle, saying she needed something backstage, resulting in a hasty dash, and quick change into costume, to take my position with the other lads at the side of the stage.

The music started and, as part of the plan, the original team took their position on stage, a few seconds later and the music stopped, suggesting a problem had occurred, then as they walked off stage left, with the accompanying music of Eminems';

"Guess who's back, back again, guess who's back, guess who's back"

And a photo on the stage background of the Dance Dads Amy.

Enter stage right those said, dancing dads, surrounded by cheers of realisation, an eruption of excitement and anticipation, we took up our positions. We danced, we performed, we did well, it has to be said, this performance was better than our first, it was more controlled, and it was only three minutes!

In fact, here you go; you watched the first time around, take an opportunity to watch our latest offering...
https://www.youtube.com/watch?v=E6iysvNTsJc

When the curtain closed on our performance, to the background of loud applause, I remember with much fondness, Danielle's reaction, she ran across the stage and jumped at me, straddling me, giving me the biggest hug ever, that one single moment, that one hug, it made everything feel worthwhile, from the crazy idea in the first place, our first outing, to now, at the end of our latest jaunt.

It felt a little strange too, that the shoe was on the other foot, normally I'd be the one watching her, I'd be the one savouring that feeling of bursting pride that I was so lucky to experience so often when I watched her dance, but tonight it was her turn, and she felt it, that night, and I felt her feel it, her dad had done her proud, we all had, the dance dads army did her proud!

We did ourselves proud, not just with the performance, but from day one, the effort we invested, the commitment we gave, we worked hard, granted, even at the end of the journey, we are still dads dancing, but we did our best, and I shall take this opportunity to publicly thank those other dads,

"Gentlemen, it was a true honour to share your company every

week at rehearsals, and in sharing our time on that stage together,

thank you, it was amazing, because you all made it so, cheers!!"

There was actually another outing, one normally left unspoken of, within the dads dance camp. But, were I to omit its existence in this chapter, it would lead to much criticism from certain factions within the school.

This performance nestles between the two shows, it was actually our second 'live' performance, the anniversary show, our third.

The school had entered a competition, and amongst the many sections available, there was one dedicated to the parents. Yes there was a section open to parents, and we dads, as experienced dancers, qualified.

We had wanted to use what we had already learnt, performed, there wasn't enough time ahead of the competition, to start from afresh, learn a new routine, and given that very few sections allow dances of over eleven minutes in length, we were going to have to butcher the routine, and get it down to three minutes.

Yes, agreed, if only Ian had stuck to the original plan!

And so, we cut the music and the routine, patching it up to meet the criteria, for the length of the song. It threw us, you're suddenly following a certain move with a different one, and it made it difficult.

So when we came to doing the competition, the new routine wasn't as deep-seated in our psyche, as it might have been. Now the speaker system at the venue left much to be desired, it just wasn't loud enough, as you can imagine, I had my own very strong views about that fact.

The result, once we started dancing and the audience started to make a noise, I couldn't hear, now I know this might be sounding like an attempt at making excuses, and it is, I need an excuse!

Because to my horror, at one point, I couldn't hear the music, leaving me, watching the others and trying to keep up, and failing quite miserably.

Now the thing about performing in a show is that you're not being judged, well obviously, ultimately you are, but not like here, here there were marks, given at the end. Yes, we were to be judged, and the verdict would be made public in the placings.

I needn't have worried my pretty little face, not for one minute, as the results were announced, revealing that we had, in fact, secured second place, runners-up!

Well, last place if you're going to be more specific, yes, there had only been the two entries, and to make matters worse, much worse, unbelievably worse.

The victorious team, the winners, the ones that had secured first place, was a team of dance mums.

From Ktz Dance!

Yes, we had been beaten by our nemesis, the mums from our school, things don't get any worse than that, and that my friends, is why it is never spoken of, in the dads camp at least, you can imagine the mums camp, they were banging on about little else for weeks after!

Anyway, no bad feelings;

"Well Done Ladies"

Dance Dads Army, in case you're wondering, just how the name originated, well, in the early days of our first rehearsals, I was sat at home and an episode of the popular series from bygone years

'Dads Army' was on the TV.

I watched, and witnessed these old men, way past their best, buffooning their way through moments of pure chaos, accompanied by witty one liners and quips, yet no matter how hard they endeavoured to get things right, they succeeded only in creating scenes of disorder and disarray, so in truth, the name pretty much wrote itself, we were

The 'Dance Dads' Army

Now, onto the most obvious of questions;

Will there be another outing?

Who knows!

We say no, but in truth.....you never really say never!

In fact, last year we were approached by the research team of Simon Cowells latest venture ' *The Greatest Dancer*', they, having seen the video on YouTube, saw us as a potential novelty act, not actual dancers, never mind greatest dancers, we offered something in the way of entertainment.

I spoke at length with one of the researchers, giving a full background to the team, Danielle and the dance school, they sounded interested, but alas, that's as far as it went, it transpired that there was another dance dads team selected to appear, so one would assume they got our spot, watching them, and the reaction they got, I felt a small tinge of regret that we hadn't been given the opportunity, we could have certainly have competed on a level with those other dads, but as always with those talent programmes, it all comes down to a good 'sob' story, and they had one, we didn't.

"I'm not bitter, just twisted!"

CHAPTER 5 – HOLLY

*"The better I get to know men, the
more I find myself loving dogs"*

Charles De Gaulle

N ow, I'm sneaking this little chapter in, admittedly this section has absolutely no connection to dance, so if you're not a doggy kind of person, I suggest you possibly just fast-forward, and jump ahead, straight to the next chapter.

During a large portion of the time that I've covered in this book, our family had another member, and to omit her from the proceedings, would seem like a betrayal of her existence, so I introduce you to our dog, not just any dog, I might add, you see she was *'the'* dog,

I'll be honest, having never had a dog before, I was a little naive in understanding the attraction of them, I could never grasp the owner's obsession with them, it was a dog, just a dog.

Danielle and Ben had asked for years for one, don't all kids? But I was always resolute, defiant in my decision not to have one, but as they grew a little older, that weakened. And in truth, I got a little soft in my old age.

I spoke about it with Pam, who in all honesty was more excited by the prospect that even the kids were. And with that we made the decision that for Christmas we were going to bless them with a dog.

I had stipulations though, it was going to have to be a dog from a 'clever' breed, the thought of a 'thick' dog filled me with dread, and the little 'yappy' ones, I didn't like them, so they were out of the reckoning too.

Based on those two requirements, research led us to believe that the most suitable choice was to be a Border Collie, so off we went in search, we located a place between Bolton and Bury, a farm that bred them, and that is when we first met her, picking her out almost instantly, me because I liked her colouring, Pam because it looked like this puppy was getting bullied by its brother, she felt sorry for it.

We were to return, late on Christmas Eve to collect her, and she would spend the night, secretly, hidden away in the Conservatory. I have no idea how we pulled it off, keeping it a secret from Danielle and Ben until Christmas morning, but we did.

I will never forget their reactions, their faces that morning, as that little puppy greeted them, bounding into the room excitedly. They were in total shock, I had been adamant in my refusal in the past, so they held no expectation that might ever change, but now, here in front of their very eyes was a puppy, our puppy.

Now the first job was to grant her a name, well actually, the first job was to clean up all the urine that she had sprayed all over the floor, so the second job, was to grant her...., hold that thought, that job was now picking up the poo that she had just deposited on the living room floor....

The tenth job that morning, was to grant her a name, and being Christmas Day, well it made it easy;

Holly, our very own Christmas Holly.

◆ ◆ ◆

Now in hindsight we hadn't needed to bother with presents for them that year, they had all they wanted in this little ball of black and white fur, it was late in the evening when the last of the presents even got unwrapped, and none of them held any comparison with the new addition to our family.

I had a strict set of rules regarding her;

Treats, they had to be earned, not given frivolously, that lasted until about the same time as I finished the sentence.

She would not be allowed upstairs, no, I was adamant about that, until ten minutes later, when she was in fact, upstairs.

Beds, furniture, she would not be allowed on any of those, as you might have guessed, pretty much all those rules had gone by the time we woke on Boxing Day morning.

Now being honest, in that early time, at the beginning, I struggled. I found it so hard, frustrating, and the biggest reason for that was the fact that I could not reason with her, explain things, as you can when raising children, offer a story, morals. But the more I spent time with her, the more I looked into those eyes, the more I realised, that her love was unconditional. Never, not one time did I not return home, to find her excited, pleased to see me.

Very soon, she had taken her place within the family, and she understood that there was a hierarchy, and she soon realised that her place was at the top. We merely worked for her

Pam's role was to feed her.

Danielle was her playtime buddy.

Ben was her confidante.

And I, well I was the one who took her for walks.

And I took that role very seriously, my days off spent walking miles, for hours on end, exploring.

And over the years we grew closer, Danielle used to marvel in the fact that Holly had won me over, she thought it cute. And in truth it was, I never thought I was capable of that level of attachment to an animal.

But it comes at a price, and I think you already know what is to come.

So I shall give you fair warning, there is little in the way of fun, humour or little witty anecdotes in the next section.

Just like the rest of the book, I hear you say.

We had started to notice things weren't just right, her appetite suddenly increasing by the day, yet weight falling from her just as quickly, she seemed constantly thirsty, waking us during the night for a drink, her urine had taken on a pungent, strong odour, and there was an increase in its regularity.

You know deep down inside that it isn't good, but denial makes attempts at protecting you, convincing you that it's probably something small, worms or a small infection.

But when the vet gave us the news, in truth it held little surprise to us, she was diagnosed with diabetes, that day was a Friday, and the vet had outlined our options, which in truth wasn't even options, not viable ones at least, and there was only the one option, the final option. He had suggested we didn't leave it long, suggesting that the beginning of the following week was the most appropriate time, but if things developed we could take her to the emergency clinic they held over the weekend.

It was devastating news, the worst news, how were we going to tell Danielle and Ben. I have to confess it was one of the most difficult times of my life, but as an adult, a dad, you have to wear a strong face.

That night I drove her to one of our favourite walking spots, I watched her, yes, she had become frail in her appearance, but she seemed full of youthful exuberance, running around the woods, it didn't feel right that this might be the last walk we shared.

On the car journey back home, I allowed her to ride shotgun, sat the on passenger seat, it was her first time.

I drove, distracted, constantly glancing across to her, she was loving every minute of it, it looked like she felt like a princess, honoured with her new seat, her throne. She did that thing, that dogs do, that makes it look like they are smiling, but she wasn't just smiling, she was grinning from ear to ear.

On my return, I spoke to Pam, there was no way we could take the dog, that I had just witnessed for the last hour or so, bounding around the woods, sat so happily beside me in the car, to the vets that following Monday.

We didn't know just how long we had left with her, but I was damn sure it surpassed a couple of days.

It transpired that we were blessed with her for a further two weeks, deteriorating slowly but surely, to that point that it would not have been fair, or humane to allow it to continue.

We made the decision to take her to her appointment at the vets together, as a family.
I don't know to this day, if that was the right decision, I'd never been there before or since, but that was the decision we took.

So on that fateful Tuesday, on Ben's return from school, we all got in the car, and made the most silent of journeys to the vets.
If you, yourself, have been in a similarly unfortunate and sad situation, you will realise there are no words, none.

Just as there is no reason, to dwell on the events, that took place at the vets, in the writing of this book.

It was a traumatic time for us all, as a family, we were all devastated but it hit Ben the hardest, we knew it would, together they had formed a strong bond, as I said earlier, Ben was her confidante, she was at her most relaxed with him, they would lie together, I always presumed, sharing things, talking without words.

For days, weeks following that day, Ben took with him, wherever he went, Hollys ball, he would sit watching TV with it in his hand, it was in his bag when he went to school, and to this day, it sits, taking pride of place on his bedside table.

As with any bereavement, time heals, not fully, never completely, but it helps in easing the pain of those first days, when the pain is raw, fresh.

But every now and then, you get hit, when you're least suspecting of it, and it will take you down at the knees.

One such occasion, was last Christmas Day, Danielle now earning a wage had bought us all presents, I was on the opposite side of the room when Ben ripped the wrapping paper from his, I couldn't actually see the present itself, but I saw his reaction to it. He was genuinely appreciative, and thanked Danielle with such appreciation I was intrigued to find out what it was.

As it was passed to me, the realisation of what it was hit me, Danielle had taken photo's that we had of Ben and Holly together, and had sent them away to be transformed into one of those personalised photo-books.

I would have preferred a little warning, to gather myself. I'd been handed the book, so I had to look through it, Pam could see my face, she watched as I flicked through the pages, my bottom lip trembling, tears rolling down my cheek;

"Bloody Dog!"
Making me cry, like that…. like this.

And so there you have, as I said I couldn't write a book and not give her the mention she so fully deserved.

I didn't forget you Holly, you got your time, your place in this book.
We will never forget you!
Rest in Peace, Good Girl

CHAPTER 6 – CAREERS

"Choose a job you love, and you will never have to work a day in your life"
-Confucius-

I had absolutely no idea who this Confucius chap was, so I researched him, well I say researched; I looked him up on Wikipedia, same difference really!

It transpires that he was a Chinese philosopher and politician from around 500BC, who is famed for his many inspirational quotes.

There has been a recent online trend on social media to attribute some, in my opinion, equally inspirational, albeit more tongue in cheek ramblings to him, such as;

> *'Baseball wrong, man with four balls unable to walk'*

And my particular favourite;

> *'It is only when a mosquito lands on your testicle, that you realise that there is always a way to solve a problem without using violence'*

Be honest, how profound is that!

So back to the original quote, choose a job you love, an inspirational quote indeed, and so very true!

As I'm writing this, Danielle is half way through a contract as a dancer on the Island of Rhodes, one of the Greek Dodecanese Islands, bathed in sunshine, boasting such natural beauty and surrounded by breathtaking landscapes, there is a relaxed, tranquil ambience to the place, and two weeks ago we were lucky enough to be enjoying all that the island had to offer.

This was our first visit to this Island and I had instantly fallen in love with the place, our only previous experience of the Dodecanese was a holiday to the Island of Kos a number of years ago, ironically Danielle joined us on that trip, albeit as a tiny little, baby bump.

I say tiny!

But who am I trying to kid, Pam was massive when she was pregnant, I'm surprised the plane even managed to get off the ground, but don't ever tell her, that I told you that.

Since writing this, Pam has proof read it and insisted, well demanded to be more specific, upon its removal, so I apologise, but it has to go, that said, it's actually highly unlikely she's ever going to read it again, surely.

I think I'll risk it, take a chance, it can stay, just don't tell her!

The Dodecanese, translated/meaning twelve islands, in the south-eastern Aegean Sea, is a group of twelve large Greek islands known for their medieval castles, Byzantine churches, beaches and ancient archaeological sites, Rhodes is the largest and boasts wonderful views of neighbouring Turkey, Danielle is based in Ialysos, Ixia, a popular beach resort with stunning coastal views and a friendly local charm.

"Ian, this isn't a travel guide, on with the story please!"

Ok, so she's there, she has a six month contract over the summer months, with an Entertainments Agency providing nightly dance shows at two hotels on the Island.

Both stunning hotels;

The Mitsis Alila Resort, located just a short distance from Faliraki, an exceptionally beautiful hotel overflowing with opulence, a place exclusively reserved for only the most affluent of holidaymaker, evaluated by Danielle on her first visit as;

"This place is like a Royal Palace"

And it was, the grandeur of the architecture, the majestic décor, it was a place of ultimate luxury, however, that said, it was a little too much so for my liking, put simply, a bit too posh for lil ole me!

I noticed, on watching the *'kids club'* that preceded the dance show there one night, how the children hadn't seemed like children at all, they were more like young adults, it was a little surreal, to see a group of children, ranging in ages from two to ten, assembled together, on holiday, yet all sitting there, waiting, patiently, for the start.

Well I can only assume that their nannies and butlers had done the most amazing of jobs in raising them.

The other hotel;

The Akti Imperial Deluxe Resort and Spa, located in Ixia, just a thirty minute walk from Danielle's accommodation, which we were blessed to call our home for the following week.

A week of five star, all-inclusive luxury, it was much more relaxed, comfortable, and whilst still boasting an air of elegance, it had none of the pomp, and the cherry on the top, we got to watch all the shows!

The first of which was underway on our touchdown on the runway tarmac, culminating in a mad dash to the hotel, luckily situated, just a short ten minute drive from Diagoras Airport.
We had initially been a little fortuitous, with a tail wind shortening our flight time, resulting in us landing earlier than anticipated, however, unfortunately we had landed just after a Russian Airlines flight, and for some reason, of which I am unaware, it takes much longer for them to pass through passport control and security, the knock on effect causing a hindrance to our anticipated swift passage.

As I say, I have no idea why it should take longer for Russian passengers to exit, but our, presumably, very knowledgeable, taxi driver Stavros, informed us, of that fact.

Now I don't actually know his name, in fairness, that's because I never actually went to the effort to ask him, but to me, he looked like a Stavros, so much so that if it isn't Stavros, he should seriously think about changing it.

Now at this point I will take the opportunity to apologise to all the people in that queue at passport control who we very cheekily, by sneaking past a barrier, pushed in front of, it's really not in our nature, we're normally very *'British'* in that respect, but we were on a mission, a race against time, action that I felt was justified on this one special occasion.

A speedy check in at the hotel reception before hastily heading towards the outdoor stage area, excitement building, the volume of the music increasing on our approach, overwhelming anticipation growing with each hurried step, rounding the corner of the building, we caught our first glimpse of the stage, surrounded by seats packed with the on looking audience.

I had the urge to run, to sprint forward, get there as quick as I could, but glancing ahead I noticed Danielle wasn't actually on the stage at that particular moment, so my steps eased and we reached the seating area in good time, searching out three free seats, it didn't matter which, it mattered only that we were there, and we took our seats, with emotions running high, as you'd expect.

And then, suddenly, there she was, striding out onto the stage to the background of the next song, bursting with a plethora of emotions, a combination of joy, excitement, elation, pride, I could feel the wide smile stretching across my face, the like of which results in your jaw aching.

Following weeks of being separated from her, and believe me, those weeks felt like years, she was there, in front of me, I could finally see her, true enough, over those previous weeks, we'd chatted on Facetime, spoken at length on the phone, but this was different, this was real, we were to be reunited, albeit briefly, but for the next week we could share her company, her experiences, this beautiful location and the life she was living.

We sat there and enjoyed what remained of the show, torn between wanting the show to last longer, prolonging the enjoyment, the immense feeling of pride that I always revel in when watching her perform, and wanting it to end so she could come and see us.

As I savoured, what was undoubtedly going to prove to be the Finale, I knew that moment was close, I clapped enthusiastically as I watched her take her bows, her applause, the adulation of the audience.

And then, as she turned and took her steps to head backstage, well that moment wasn't just close now, it was here, finally!

It was 24 degrees that evening and she'd been dancing under lighting for an hour and a half, she was drenched in sweat, soaking, still in costume, but it didn't detract from how special that first hug felt, I didn't care that my arms were wrapped around sweaty, sodden flesh, that her costume, soaked with that said sweat was pressed against my new, crisp, white *'holiday'* shirt, it mattered only, that I was getting the hug I had missed and craved for so many weeks, and it felt good, so incredibly good!

It was touching, also to see the excitement on the faces of the other dancers, they to still in full costume, hurriedly joining Danielle in greeting us, they gave us the warmest of welcomes, you could see the genuine pleasure of meeting us across their beaming faces, and so they to, got sweaty hugs, and they to, were worth it.

When your daughter is almost two thousand miles away, in a foreign country, it is, for any parent, a cause for worry, a time of apprehension. In your mind she is out there alone, vulnerable, away from the home, it's comforts and it's stability, and you become reliant on the people she is living with, spending her time with, to offer that that same stability and those same comforts.

It became instantly apparent to us, upon meeting those other dancers that we had no reason to worry any longer, we had absolutely no cause for concern, for in those three individuals, those three special people, beautiful on the inside and out, she had found not only colleagues, not just roommates, not ordinary dance partners, she had found friends, friends for life, she had found her *'Rhodes family'*

It was evident, having just watched them dance together, that they had become close, and not just in the fluidity of the routines, but those knowing glances, cast across the stage to each other, that only they understood.

Over the course of the following week we would see just how close they had in fact become, as we saw them living their lives together, not just colleagues working together, but friends, sharing almost every minute of every day together, and it was clear to see how just how happy, how relaxed, content, they were, as that family.

Pasquale, an Italian guy with immense experience of a long career in dance, he was Danielle's roommate on her arrival for the first couple of weeks.

When I think of the day she travelled out there, waking that morning, in the sanctuary of her home, with her family around her, then a mere twelve hours, just half a day later, sat alone, in her new accommodation, awaiting the return of the other dancers from that nights show, strangers, people she was destined to spend the next six months with.

It must have felt so very daunting, intimidating, but as she sat there, she held in her hand, a note, left on her bed, from Pasquale, and it was the most beautiful of notes.

I will be forever indebted to him for the way in which he welcomed her in those first few days, not only with that first note, but on offering advice, support and assurances, and for that I am eternally grateful;

"Molto grazie, amico mio!"

Beth and Heather, the two girls, they too got a big thumbs up from me, quite literally Beth!

Now I'm fully aware, that statement, in isolation, will make no sense to any of you whatsoever, it is in fact, a private little joke, between myself and the girls.

But, you're walking alongside me on this journey, so I will share with you, that private little private joke, divulging the reason behind its existence.

During our time over there, we had taken a trip to visit a Waterpark, located in Faliraki, the two girls, Heather and Beth, had taken the opportunity to join us on our little excursion.

We had the most amazing of days there, the rides, or more accurately our experiences on them, had prompted much laughter during the course of the day.

We had taken a break for lunch, with me ordering a traditional Greek Gyros, now being cheaply priced, I had assumed, that the Gyros was going to be a mini-version, and with me having worked up quite the appetite, what with my hurtling down ride after ride on the park, and running, literally, from one to the next. So, in my wisdom I decided it best to order a portion of chips as a side.

Soon the food arrived at our table, my 'full sized' extra-large Gyros, accompanied by a bucket of chips!

I was pleasantly surprised, I mean, normally, food outlets at places like these, traditionally work out quite expensive affairs, a trip to Blackpool Pleasure Beach or Alton Towers, and you end up spending as much on the food as you did on the entry fee.

But, this place was setting a shining example, excellent food, at reasonable prices, resulting in exceptional value. I mean, surely these places would sell more, if they kept their priced down.

Now, for all its value, the food had a down-side, and that

was, that I was now sitting, dried off, full and feeling a little lethargic, the lure of all those exhilarating rides holding little interest. Luckily, Danielle has visited the park on a previous occasion, and had experienced the very same thing. So, with experience, comes knowledge, and as they say, knowledge is power. We followed her advice, her perfect plan, and headed off to the 'Lazy River' ride.

Let me explain further, we mounted our inflatable rings, and entered the water, where a soft current would then send us on a relaxing journey around the outskirts of the park, located high up a big hill, it offered the most amazing views of the surrounding landscape. Basking in thirty degree heat, the sun beating down on us, we enjoyed the most relaxing of experiences, and by the end, we were re-vitalised, refreshed, and ready to take on the challenges of the bigger, faster, and indeed steeper rides.

We were having the best day, but close to the end of the afternoon, we stumbled across the best ride, the ride of all rides, which is a strange thing to say, given it isn't actually a ride, allow me to explain.

The 'Wet Bubble', as its name suggests, is a domed structure with a fountain at the peak, that supplies a steady stream of water cascading down the surface of the dome, added to the fact that this makes it very slippery, it's also, very bouncy, lending itself well to every opportunity of making a variety of fun filled descents to the bottom, culminating with splash landing, into the surrounding moat.

I suspect that over here, it would fail every Health and Safety inspection going, based on the potential for danger and injury, and I mean lethal injury, broken necks and the like.

But that aside, it was fun, now to make the ascent to the top, there were ropes descending downwards from the top, and these were used to climb upwards.

Now this is the point where the thumb enters proceedings, literally.

So imagine, I'm excitedly clambering up the robe, in a rush to reach the top, Beth just inches in front of me, my hands gripping the rope tightly, thumbs pointing forward, leading the way.

It was at this point that I became distracted, Danielle, on a rope to the left of us, slipped, causing her to lose grip on her rope, resulting in the most unceremonious of descents, it was hilarious, reflected in the outburst of laughter from us all. I continued with my climb....but Beth didn't, she stopped, and with my vision focused on Danielle to my left, well, my thumb....

Entered more than just the proceedings!

"To Infinity and Beyond!"

To be fair Beth took it well.
I should maybe re-phrase that actually, it sounded like a review, a judgement on her ability to.....
I feel like I'm making this worse now.
She took it...... no, I can't start a sentence with those words.
Beth.........I can't, it seems that there is no word I can use that doesn't lend itself well to a double entendre, so I'll keep it simple.

Beth didn't call the Police.

The moment was taken in good humour, I apologised, many, many times, and she was fine with it, she found it funny, and it has now made it into the halls of fame, something we joke about a lot.

So imagine my horror just a couple of hours later, at the end of the day, all dried off, changed and relaxing outside the café, eating lollies and ice creams.

Beth was seated next to me, I assume in keeping with the quote from the 'Godfather' film;

"Keep your friends close"
"And your enemies closer"

Ben was seated to the other side of me, his discarded lolly wrapper on the table in front of us, as I sat, still licking my wounds of embarrassment from the earlier incident, fate decided, in its wisdom, that there was still a little fun to be had.

It had been a sunny, still day weather wise, up until that point, but from somewhere came a little breeze, just a fleeting transient, momentary breeze, just enough to blow the discarded lolly wrapper. As it took flight, I instinctively reached out in an effort to catch it. Now the direction in which it could have blown was, you would think, totally random, but no.

It headed straight in the direction of Beth's bikini clad chest.
Now was Beth, aware of the wrapper, No.
Was Beth aware of my hand, lurching swiftly towards her chest.
Yes, yes indeed she was, I could tell by the look on her face, in her eyes, that look of fear when someone feels threatened, on the verge of impending assault.

Now, I'm certainly no litter lout.
Sexual predator, yes, evidently, but definitely not a litter lout, but on that occasion, I pulled my arm back, and I let that lolly wrapper fly off to wherever it wanted to be.

And Beth, well, she has since retracted the injunction and restraining order, and the courts have granted me escorted visits, so all seems good again.

On the subject of my thumbs, I have a further revelation; for my trusted thumbs, my chosen weapon of assault, are flawed, I have an actual condition, and it has an actual name, that I will share with you;

'Brachydactyly Type D'

Now it's not, as you might assume by its name, the name of an extinct, long forgotten flying dinosaur, it's a condition, often referred to in a number of other ways;
'stubbed thumb'
'club thumb'
'royal thumb'
'murderers thumb'
'thumb toe'

It is a clinically recognised condition, where the thumbs are relatively short and round, with an accompanying wide nail bed, basically my thumbs are about a third shorter than the considered norm, yet wider.

So, to sum up;

'What I lack in length, I make up for in girth'

And that's pretty much how Beth had described how it had felt at the time!

I'll be honest, when I set about writing this book, that sentence was not one I could have ever anticipated having to write!

Now I'm not on my own with this thumb condition, although it is relatively rare, affecting approximately nought point five percent of the population. One of those affected is Megan Fox, the American Actress and Model, incredulously, there are a number of Instagram pages out there dedicated to them, check them out.

Now, having these thumbs can impact quite significantly on life, and that's not me being a drama queen here, I mean let's hope I never break down when I'm out in the car, because I suspect I would not have a successful career in hitch-hiking, drivers would just miss-interpret the situation, thinking I was just waving a fist at them, more likely to result with a punch rather than a lift.

Ten pin bowling, now they do have balls that have a hole big enough to accommodate these most special of digits, however, it would need the strength of ten men to physically lift the bloody thing!

I spoke earlier in a chapter regarding my inability to play a musical instrument, that wasn't due to not wanting to, not trying to learn, I did, we had a keyboard at home, I was fine with my fingers, but when I came to use my thumb, well, it just didn't reach, and if I moved my whole body around to reach, its width resulted in me pressing two keys!

Texting, using my thumb, that's a no no, the wide pad of my thumb resulting in multiple keys being pressed at the same time, leaving a series of random mixed up letters in place of legible words, and having to then use an index finger instead, leading people to assume, believe this fact is due to incompetence rather than disability.

Now when people see these thumbs for the first time, you have to prepare yourself, you will be looked upon as a kind of freak show act, with them continually asking to see those bad boys, not only that, every person you meet whilst in the company of that individual, will be prompted to also look.

And when you meet a fellow sufferer, someone also cursed with the same affliction, there is an instant bonding, like your both members of a select group, exchanging stories, experiences, I often feel that we should establish an official group, unite all our fellow 'Brachydactylyites' appointing Megan Fox as our leader, in fact I'll send her a quick text now;

'Gt jkmrefgza lrdfvgui iou jhn lpk rduhu'

Bloody Thumbs!

Now you might feel I have been a tad unlucky to have been born with a condition affecting my thumbs, but oh no, I was unluckier than that, the condition also affecting my big toes, which in truth aren't actually my big toes, no, that title is reserved for my index toe, if there is such a thing, the second toe in, the one next to the 'big toe'.

In my case, that toe is in fact the longest, now when you look at my toes, that one appears similar to ET's finger, long, towering, exposed, and it has a purpose, a role, its job being to re-arrange all the furniture in my house, yes, I bang it a lot! I get it caught under my foot, it is very injury prone.

I once broke my big toe playing football, and I went to have an x-ray at the hospital, I started to become a little concerned, when doctor after doctor would come to examine my digit, it would result in them staring intently at it, then staring at the x-ray, before a shake of the head, and off they would pop.

Only to return soon after, with another doctor, who would then repeat the process, until finally one of those doctors, a logical one, asked me to remove the sock from my other foot, my uninjured one, before pointing and declaring to all the other doctors that;

*"The other ones exactly the same, that's just how
his toes are, its normal for him"*

My toe had caused much confusion and deliberation, to look at it, it appeared to have been shunted, as if I had crushed the bone, shortening its appearance, yet a look at the x-ray was revealing no more than a simple break.

So there you have it, you are now aware of my very own little, genetic mutation, and the fact that I have five items that can be considered short and stumpy!
Give it a minute, think about it, the penny will drop soon enough, five?

Anyway, that was quite the digression, who knew that a simple sexual assault on a young girl I had only recently met, would lead to such an extensive part of this chapter.

So, the girls. Heather came from Scotland and was the Dance Captain, and she was a dancer with great technique and energy, she was a pleasure to be around, really good company.

Beth, who had lived in Ireland and Lancashire, leaving her with an accent that, to me at least, resembled that of a Cornish Farmer at times, she was a natural performer, a good dancer who interacted well with the audience.

I'm told she also has the most amazing vocal ability to, so destined possibly for a big future in Musical Theatre, she certainly has the stage presence to succeed. She to, was a pleasure to be around, she was funny, with a contagious laugh and a great sense of humour.

Over the course of the following week we spent a lot of time in the company of those two, and it was, indeed, a true pleasure, that infamous, fun visit to the Water Park in Faliraki, culminating in what was ,for every one of us, victims included, the most amazing fun day out, we had many trips to the beach with them, spent time at their accommodation, we shared great times and many laughs, Ben enjoyed their company, and they seemed to enjoy his.

Especially when witnessing the occasion, on which he got drunk, yes drunk, when celebrating his 15th birthday.

We were sharing after show drinks with the both of them and Pasquale,
I was enjoying my vodka, Pam was enjoying her vodka, Danielle was enjoying her cocktail and Ben…

Well, Ben was enjoying our vodkas and cocktail to!

With us all engrossed in a particularly competitive game of Uno, Ben seized upon our distraction to help empty our glasses, the result, random glassy eyed stares combined with unprovoked giggling, he was in a happy place, but his Uno skills were severely affected, normally so ponderous in the placing of a card, it was now replaced with aimless hurling of his card onto the pile followed by an arbitrary bout of laughter, and his walk to the toilets, when he seemed to be putting in doubt the Confucius theory regarding man's ability to walk with four balls!

It was his birthday and he was in a wonderful setting, with wonderful people and he was having the most wonderful of times.
Soon after he was in our wonderful room with his wonderful head in a wonderful bin, recycling that wonderful vodka, alcohol, it's a learning curve, only, we never ever really learn do we, whatever our age.

And whilst the episode probably puts in jeopardy my sequel book;

'Responsible Parenting Volume One'

I am kind of pleased that his first drunken episode was in our presence and not down some back alley with his mates.

We had the most amazing week out there with Danielle, and thank you Pasquale, Heather and Beth, you played a massive part in that, you are both special talents with undoubtedly, amazing careers ahead, and it was a pleasure to share your company and we all consider you as special friends of our family.

I take a pause from writing to glance through the window here, it's dull, miserable, raindrops cascading over the glass of the window like tears, weeping down a sculptured cheek, there are dark clouds above, holding the promise of a further, imminent downpour, the cool blustery wind belies the fact that it's mid-August, it's supposed to be summer for God's sake!

The sun, hiding, with its fleeting attempts, vain efforts to peek from behind the black clouds, ultimately in vain.

The vision mirrors my mood as I reflect on my recent trip, ponder, ahead of the twelve hour shift that awaits me tonight, the prospect filling me with more than a little dread and trepidation.

It's not that I hate my job, it's just not how I would choose to spend my evening, but it's what pays the bills, it's what I have to do, it's what we all have to do, we have jobs, and we work them, and tonight I will turn up on shift, and it will come, and it will go, and when questioned by Pam in the morning on how the shift was, I will reply simply "it came, and it went"

Two weeks ago, I was basking in the sun, enjoying the local friendly charm offered by the good people of Rhodes, to give an example of that friendly charm; I will share a little story with you.
We had taken a taxi journey from Rhodes Town, back to our

hotel in Ixia, we'd done it before, it normally cost 8 euros, the taxi driver, Nikos, a seemingly friendly chap, yes, you guessed right, I have no idea of his name either, but he suited Nikos, so there we go.

Nikos engaged us in conversation, enquiring if this was our first visit to Rhodes, if we liked it, was having a good time, the standard questions really, he asked if we had had the opportunity yet, to savour the sights of the Acropolis, now being honest, I didn't even know what the Acropolis was, never mind the fact of its location here on the Island, so I informed him, that unfortunately, we hadn't had chance yet, but it was on our list, to which he replied;

"I will take you now, it's just a slight diversion, we can go that way back to the hotel, it's a little longer journey, but it will be worth it!"

Now, when you get to my age, especially given my profession, you hold a certain level of cynicism, borne from life and its everyday bumps and scrapes, it leaves you constantly wary, suspecting.

So I was very well aware of what was unfolding here, he was pulling a fast one on us, preying on our vulnerability as first time visitors, the ten minute journey was presumably, to transform into an hours journey, with the cost, I suspected, to at least triple.

Well, I wasn't falling for that con trick, I would just, politely, but firmly, tell him to take the normal route.

But as I said before, I can be very *'British'* at times;

"Thank you, Nikos, that will be wonderful!"

And, so, we headed up in to the hills, I mean it didn't matter really, yes, it would cost more, a lot more, probably, but it's just those euro thingies, monopoly money, that's what happens when you are on holiday, away from the familiarity of the pound note, those euros, well, they hold no real value, do they.

*"30 euros Nikos, of course, here take an extra
10 for yourself my good man"*

We drove past the Acropolis, but from a distance, now, given that the distance was quite significant, to offer any feedback would prove difficult, I couldn't, reliably, verify if they are worth seeing or not from the vantage point we held, but Nikos appeared very excited about it all.

Our drive then came to the most abrupt of stops, Nikos suddenly breaking hard, his facing sporting the most mischievous of smiles, before announcing, very dramatically, in my opinion;

"Everybody out!"

Flinging open his door, which he then left wide open, as he quickly headed to the edge of the hillside;
"Come, come," beckoning us to follow him"
"Follow me, you have one minute, just one minute! That is all!"

Just one minute?
For what?
To live? I presumed!

I was becoming fairly sure these events were leading up to our impending demise, I just didn't know just how yet, but that wasn't important, and besides, it gave me a little something to look forward to, a little something to occupy my mind in those last few moments of life.

So, in our very *'British'* manner, we followed his instruction, decamped from the vehicle, and followed him, to what I assumed, would be certain death.

Casting a glance, back over my shoulder, at the taxi, it looked surreal, parked erratically at the side of a dirt track, at the peak of this tall cliff, empty, but with all four doors flung wide open, and the engine still running, in fact, all that seemed missing from this bizarre, ghostly scene was the blue and white, *'police-do not cross'*, tape.

But, no need to worry, as that would, no doubt, come soon!

"Look, Look,"

Screamed Nikos, with much excitement.

His words echoing in the surrounding mountains, startling me, making me jump, that's never good a thing, for an acrophobic, already consumed with a feeling of impending doom, perched at the edge of a precipice, no, making him jump, that's not good at all.

"Just one minute to look"

He repeated, his voice, now, verging on hysteria.

I looked up, in trepidation, expecting to be met by the sight of the barrels of a shotgun, staring back, straight towards me.

"See, that beautiful view, enjoy it, for you only
have one minute, then we must go"

The view, if only there words, that could describe it, but sadly, there are none that could do it justice, it was beautiful, clear skies, the sun setting over the clear blue sea, its rays glimmering across the gentle waves, it truly was a magnificent view, and one to behold.

And we had our minute, just one minute, as he had promised, with such vigour, and that minute, was shared with this lovely, excitable, yes definitely excitable, but alas lovely and friendly man.

It's surprising the newfound admiration and respect, you gain for someone, the moment you realise they aren't actually Greece's most wanted and about to murder you, tossing your limp, lifeless corpse from the top of the hillside.

And so, having had our minute, savouring the view, and surviving our near death experience, we returned to the taxi, and on driving down the hill, hotel bound, I thought, whatever this taxi ride is going to cost, that view, that alone, was probably going to prove well worth it.

On the way down, Nikos spoke much of his life, his family, his time spent living on Symi Island, he truly was a lovely, warm and friendly man, and on our arrival at the hotel, he smiled, nodded in appreciation and shook my hand, I thanked him for his kind hospitality, and paid the fare, which, was 8 euros, yes, it was the same price as normal, transpires, he really did just want to show us some nice sights.

Whilst at the top of that hill, I threw over the edge, my cynicism; I didn't think I was going to have much need for it here!

The people reflected the place really, it was a tourist place of course, it's a holiday destination, but it wasn't what I would describe as touristy, if that makes sense, missing were all those 'full English breakfast' bars, with Only Fools and Horses episodes airing in the background, there was a lack of English voices, it seemed more continental, with accents from all around the world, local people walking the streets, going around their normal, everyday business, it was cosy, comfortable, friendly, and accommodating, just, as I said, like the people.

And as I say, just a fortnight ago, I was spending time here, lying on a beach, lounging by the pool, swimming in the sea.
Ok, to be fair, I don't so much swim as ....mess about, put me in water and I'm the biggest kid around, as I was busy hurtling myself into the next oncoming wave, creating a scene that can be best described as to resemble that of a shark attack,
Danielle calmly noted to Ben;
"He's very dramatic in the sea isn't he?"
To which Ben replied;
"Yeah, but then, after ten minutes he's crying that his eyes are stinging!"

Two weeks ago, I was spending the evening watching the dance shows, shows that became interactive, there were occasions during the performances that would require audience participation, and of course, who else but me was going to be chosen as a volunteer.
Now Danielle had shared the story of the *'Dance Dads Army'* in fact she had shared the YouTube footage with the other dancers, so they had high expectations of my performance on stage with them, expectations that I have to say, were not met, you see, I'd had six months rehearsals prior to our dads outing, here, the only thing I'd had prior to this performance was about six vodkas!

Two weeks ago, I was eating nice food in a beautiful setting with the most amazing views, I was relaxing, savouring the moment, I was, of course, on holiday, it's what we all do on holiday, and that's the point, Danielle is doing all those things, every day, day after day, but she's not on holiday, that is the life she is living, it's her job, it's her choice of career.

She chose a job she loves, and she does not have to work a single day of it!

Truly Inspirational indeed.

The story of how that career changed from a dream to a reality, starts as you'd expect, with a Christmas tree, allow me to explain.

Danielle, in Year 9, would have been 14 when we attended her GCSE options evening at school, on arrival we were ushered into a class room, along with other students and parents, I sat at a desk next to Danielle, with Pam on an adjoining desk.

Now, having not taken school all that seriously myself, and that said with more than a scant hint of understatement, an illustration of which was one teachers conclusion, that;

> *"If Ian put the same effort and commitment into his*
> *work that he does into trying to make people laugh,*
> *he would be a very successful student"*

I often think his words would have held more irony had I gone on to become the next stand up sensation, selling out Arena Tours, but alas, his proclamation was probably a very accurate one.

It's true, I was easily distracted, no matter how well intentioned I might have started a lesson, I would fail miserably at the first opportunity of a whispered comment, joke or laugh.

As a result I had always said, as I'm sure have so many others;

> *'If I had the chance to go back and do it all again now, I*
> *would do it all so differently, I would take it more seriously,*
> *and I wouldn't fool around'*

So why then, sat here, next to Danielle at a school desk do I feel so mischievous again, those old yearnings for a giggle flooding back!

One of the teachers began to explain how the students assembled in this room were considered the elite, the cream of the crop, the best of the best, the students holding the most promise for academic success,
I'm convinced all the other parents in the room puffed out their chest a little with pride on hearing those words about their children, how about you Ian, how exactly did you react?

You leant across to Danielle, you nudged her, then whispered, a little too loudly, given the silence filling the room;

"Pssssst, I think we're in the wrong room!"

Followed by a knowing, self-satisfied, chuckle.

Old habits die hard I guess!

But this time, unlike all those years ago, it failed to invoke a laugh, a giggle, not even a smile, this time it was met by a scathing stare, the kind of which sends a shiver down your spine, holding more impact than any words could, I felt my cheeks redden a little, and sat there like a scolded little boy, the urge to be the class clown dissolving fast.

Danielle is the one person, who with one look, can put me in my place, reign me in, maybe had she been sat at my desk all those years ago, well maybe that teachers words would have played true, maybe I would have been a successful student after all, we'll never know.

And so, the next stage of the evening, which was to go and speak with her teachers, discuss with them which subjects she should opt to take for her GCSE's, which subjects she was excelling in, which would lead to the best career options.

I should continue now with an air of modesty, as parents I suspect we are all guilty of over selling our children's ability and prowess, but in all fairness, it's hard to show that humility when teacher after teacher, gives such glowing reports on your child, amongst many other comments that evening, we were told,
"Danielle has the ability to be whatever she chooses to be"

"The only choice Danielle needs to make is, Oxford or Cambridge"

*"She can become a Doctor, a Barrister, a Vet, she has
the ability to succeed in whatever she does"*

As I said, modesty and humility, a bit of a challenge at that point.

It was a pleasure to hear such glowing comments, it seemed we had are very own, real life Lisa Simpson, and I started to think, maybe having this kid all those years ago might have been a good idea after all, maybe having to drive Pam up to the hospital with labour pains half way through the football wasn't the huge inconvenience it had seemed at the time.

I looked at Danielle and saw, for the first time, not just my little princess, not just my daughter .... I saw, a potential retirement plan!

With those thoughts we followed Danielle into 'The Street' for cake, coffee and an opportunity to discuss the evening and her options, now I should clarify, 'The Street' is an area within the school, so named because....

Well, to be honest I have no idea, no idea whatsoever, it's basically a very wide corridor, with classrooms and offices on either side.

It always bothered me why it was called that, in fact, so much so, I'm going to google the definition of *'street'*

Right, here we go;

'Street'.....

1. *a public road in a city, town, or village, typically with houses and buildings on one or both sides*
2. *relating to the outlook, values, or lifestyle of those young people who are perceived as composing a fashionable urban subculture*

Hmmm, actually, might it be that the name was deliberate, carefully chosen, an intelligent and abstract interpretation of the two definitions, its physical landscape and link to youth.

Nah, I'm sticking to my guns here, it's nothing like a street, no lampposts, no pavements, no litter, no dog shit!
See, it's nothing like a real street at all.

Now, I know what you're thinking, what about the Christmas Tree?
I'm getting to it, stay with me, we'll get there in good time.

But first, the street, the setting for what would prove a most defining moment, Pam had gone to get us all cups of coffee, leaving me and Danielle talking, discussing the comments of the teachers, it led to a conversation, and whilst it was a conversation that would set in motion the gears of Danielle's future, it's a conversation that I remember with more than a slight tinge of self-reproach.

For you see, as obvious as it was that Danielle enjoyed dance, I'd never really given consideration to the possibility of it becoming a career choice, and the last couple of hours had probably clouded that further, with talk of university, barristers and the like;

*"So, Danielle, you've heard what the teachers said,
what is it you'd really like to do as a job?"*

And without even a pause, she replied, almost instinctively;

"I want to be a dancer!"

Now this is the point that consumes me with a sense of self-loathing, my next comment, as I flippantly replied;

*"Huh, well I wanted to be a professional football, but
look at me, I drive around in a big yellow van"*

She looked up at me, not flinching, a soft smile betraying the steely determination in her eyes, the tone in her voice confident;

*"There's a difference! Because, I 'AM' going
to be a professional dancer!"*

There's a saying, I can't remember it exactly, but it's something along these lines;

'Words, like stones, once thrown, cannot be retrieved'

Now, in truth, it wasn't so much the words that were the problem, it was the sentiment, the total lack of respect, the failure to give due recognition to, and acknowledgement of, her ambition.

That's what I got so wrong, yes, it was a transient moment, short lived, and lasting only seconds, but it had a big impact on me. I felt, I should have known better.

It's painful for me to recall that conversation, even now, and this section has taken me longer to write than any other as I search for the right words, because you see, I should have known better, there was an impertinence to my response that filled me with instant regret, to suggest, even momentarily, that her aspirations of becoming a professional dancer shouldn't be taken seriously, as I said, I searched for the right words, and there's one word, the right word, the only word, abhorrent!

Took a while, but I found it eventually.

My saving grace, my redemption, was the instant realisation of my error, and if you ever throw a stone, or a wrong word, know that whilst you might not be able to retrieve it, you can, at least, bend down, pick up a little piece of humble and toss an apology over to land next to that stone or word.

I apologised at the time, and on many numerous occasions since, ironically, Danielle doesn't even remember it!
It clearly had much less of an impact on her than me, my apology at the time must have been very swift indeed.

It would have been easy to bypass that section, to just leave it out, not remember it, not write it, but that would have been unjust, I will wax lyrically about all the good things that have happened, all the positives, so it's only fair to balance that and share the lesser, negative moments.

And so, Pam returned with the drinks and the conversation continued, progressed, with positivity, and we decided we needed to formulate a plan, yes a plan,
I mean even the dancing dads had a plan, why shouldn't Danielle.

And the crux of the plan, the spine, the backbone, was, of course;

The Christmas Tree!

I feel like I might have built this up a little too much now, that you're reading with an excited anticipation, which upon I am going to fail to deliver, so help me out here, lower your expectations a little.

I had this idea, a template, a blueprint, and a framework on which to build, construct our master plan.

We needed to start at the end, and work backwards, that makes sense, surely.
The ultimate goal, success, to achieve a career in dance, performing, on stage, to become a star, and where do stars sit?

At the top of, yes, a Christmas Tree!

Pure genius this plan!

Now, imagine in your mind that tree, picture it's shape, the star sitting, shining at the top, the point, now follow that shape down, as it widens, gradually to its expansive base.

And that is where we currently stood, at the bottom looking up, looking towards the ultimate goal, the star.
The baubles hanging on the branches becoming steps on which to climb that tree and rise to the top.

So working backwards from the star, the next bauble down, what type of career was she aiming for?
Was it musical theatre, showgirl, dancing on cruises, once we knew that we could give consideration to which dance college would best provide for that specific aim, moving down the tree. See how it works?

Once you know which college you are aiming for, you can then move down the tree and see what requirements, qualifications, experiences you need to gain entry to that college.

We followed those branches down, to the point at which we were presently stood, now armed with knowledge, we had a plan, we had a Christmas Tree!

As I sit here now, I'm wondering, imagining, questioning.

Are your faces filled with the same look of total dismay, consternation, confusion that Danielle's had when I explained the tree to her?

That look of total bewilderment, suggesting my idea was not the Confucius moment I had imagined it to be.

"Ian, listen mate, let's pretend it's now the beginning of January, we've all had a good time pal, we've drank merrily, we've stuffed ourselves to bursting point with turkey, sang carols around the fire, so now, please, for god's sake"

"Put that bloody Christmas tree outside and let the bin men take it away!"

Now, having been established that, following her GCSE exams, her route would be towards performing arts and dance colleges rather than the more traditional academic routes, it was with surprise, dismay and, in Danielle's opinion, despair, that on entering her final year at school, she was selected to undertake the role as a school *'Ambassador'*

A role, which involved attendance at meetings, discussions, working to improve the school and local community.
A role, in which to be actively involved in supporting students, mentoring, providing a link between student and teaching staff.

A role, dealing with external organisations.

A role, that she needed and wanted, like a hole in the head.

She had no inclination in undertaking this position whatsoever, in truth she had little or no time in which to invest in it.

Her workload already full, every night during the week she had dance classes, a lot of the time, going straight from school, often, not to return home until after 9 o clock in the evening, Saturday mornings would be spent helping teach the little ones at the school, and there was an abundance of weekends where she would be busy attending competitions.

Her GCSEs were fast approaching and the little spare time she had, was used for revision.

As it transpired, she only attended the first two meetings, the first of which, she took as an opportunity to voice her indifference in the role, her argument, that she felt she would not benefit from all the role had to offer, and that another, more receptive student, one that would be proactive, one who would appreciate the offering, would be better suited to undertake the position.

I happen to think that she made a valid point, to some of the other students, this opportunity would have been considered invaluable, rewarding and lucrative in terms of furthering academic ambitions.

Her words, to no avail, her concerns dismissed, as she was informed, that she must continue in the role.

On a personal level, I always feel that opportunities, such as these, lend themselves better to, a process in which people can show an interest and then, in a more democratic way, be voted into the position, at least that way, the person in the role, actually wants to be involved, and thereby more likely to make it a success.

'A volunteer is worth more than ten pressed men'

Now, it wasn't just the role itself that weighed heavily on her shoulders, it was the associated attire, you see, those four selected ambassadors were identified, not by a small name badge or other subtle offering, they were distinguished by the wearing of a completely different colour of jumper.

Whilst the rest of the school year sported dark blue jumpers, the ambassadors donned purple ones, now I know that there in a little irrelevance in that, it's still jumpers, just of different colouring.

But to Danielle, it became a point of contention, as a student who had strived to pass through school life with a certain level of anonymity, seeking to blend in, not stand out, the wearing of the different colour uniform was a big issue.

I think back, to when she was in her final years at Primary School, and alongside other students, from different schools, she made the annual pilgrimage, that is *'High School Taster Day'*

A day, intended for students, to experience life in that new environment, to acclimatise to those new surroundings, to get a little taste of the syllabus, to prepare for the impending transition.

A day, that Danielle actually used as, a kind of reconnaissance mission, undertaken and performed with military precision, a preliminary survey, leading to a strategic plan, to ensure, that on that fateful first day, she would be prepared.

Not prepared in any academic sense, no.

To be prepared to fit in, not to bring attention to herself, she had taken note, not what happened in the classrooms that day, but how those older girls, already students at the school, how they dressed, wore their uniform, the length of the skirts, the style of shoes they wore, the amount of make-up they wore, every detail, even down to the their school bags, nothing of that nature, went overlooked.

It was important for her to fit in, not stand out, not just back then, but also now, and the purple jumper, well, it wasn't helping.

As a responsible parent, one of the options available to me, was to sit Danielle down, and explain the insignificance of all of this, that it mattered not, that she stood out, that it was just an item of clothing, and the person beneath that jumper was what was really important.

I chose option B.

Taking every opportunity to tease her about her inclusion in;

'The Purple Hand Gang'

It was with reference to a TV programme that Ben watched at the time, Horrid Henry.

I would pick her up from school, greeting her with, an all too familiar question;

*"So, what crazy adventures have you and the rest of
the Purple Hand Gang been up to today?"*

I envisaged that, they drove around the school, in a green and blue van, similar to that in Scooby Doo, with *'The Mystery Machine'* emblazoned across the side in big orange lettering, leaving in their midst a trail of scornful teachers, bemoaning;

> *"And I'd have got away with it, if it hadn't been for those*
> *pesky ambassadors, and their Purple Hand Gang!"*

She didn't mind, she took it with good humour, it would make her smile, distracting her away from the disdain to which she held for that single item of clothing.

Her only other attendance at those meetings, her second and final showing, was to suggest the option of moving away from the jumper idea, in favour of a small pin, or badge, I suspect, as part of her long term strategy, her plan, that she would wear that said badge for a week, maybe two, before it found its way into the depths of her school bag, destined never, to see the light of day again.
But, as with her first proposal, it was dismissed, and with that, came the end of her involvement.

I saw it as a missed opportunity, not for Danielle, but for the school, and more importantly, for another student, one who would have revelled in all the fun and adventures, that the Purple Hand Gang had to offer.

During that final year, Danielle worked towards, and sat her GCSE Exams, as it transpired, she did well, very well.
Did she do as well as she could of, had she really needed to, as well as was expected by her teachers at that options evening two years earlier, I suspect not, and to be fair, it was understandable, her true focus was elsewhere.

I'd sit with her, during revision time in her bedroom, it wasn't due to a lack of effort, or application, she would sit intently for hours, staring at pages of written words, but in truth, a lot of the time, all she saw, were the words, blah, blah, blah.

I would witness her get visibly frustrated, annoyed that those words weren't sinking in; that when I would test her, her answers would carry a tone that would suggest a question mark at the end.

As I say, had her ambition been to take the Academic route, College, University, leading to career in a chosen field, she would have found that revision much easier, because, when engaged with something, she shows a steely determination, she commits, she endeavours to succeed.
And that is why I never worried, my faith in her dreams and aspirations strong, unwavering, and as I said, she did get good marks in the end, certainly better than Mr Egg and Chips had achieved himself.

How Danielle reaches the goal of becoming a professional dancer will be touched upon in further chapters, but talking of careers, what about Ian, The Dance Dad, TheMusicIan, what about him and his career.

Well, in 1984 I left Rhyddings County High School armed only with a solitary GCSE in English Language, and very little else.

It was deserved, there's an old adage that dictates, as with anything in life, you get out, what you put in, and in all fairness I had contributed very little.

School bored me, it just didn't engage me, I saw little point in what I was being taught, it never seemed relative to life, it never felt like I was going to need any of it out in the big wide world.

I mean, yes it's very nice to hold the knowledge that in 1066 it all kicked off in a town named Hastings, that there was a bit of a punch up, resulting in some bloke losing an eye, but how was that going to help me overcome life's big hurdles,

Having that little gem of information was hardly going prove fruitful when faced with the enormity of life's big challenges, like pressing the play button on a CD player.

I wasn't a bad lad at school, I was never any trouble, I think in the main, teachers quite liked me, I was polite, courteous, approachable, I just lacked motivation to learn.

I was soon put off, take maths for example, I was fine initially, one add one is two, obviously, nine times three, twenty-seven, makes sense.
I could relate to that, I would have a use for that in later life.

Enter equations;

"So, Ian, if 3y is equal to 4a + 3b, what is 6d?"

Well, in all honesty, I couldn't give a flying....

"Egg and chips for tea tonight sir"

And negatives, how do they work.
I shall tell, they don't, they defy all common sense;

"Ian, you have 3 apples, and I'm going to take 5 of those apples away, what are you left with?"

What am I left with?
An underwhelming sense of bewilderment and dismay, that's what I'm left with!

I had three, and you managed to take five, that's a hell of a trick that is, turns out my teachers Derren Brown!

"You have minus two apples, Ian"

But no I don't, that's impossible, hear those footsteps disappearing into the distance, the door slamming shut?

That my interest, that is, and it's just left the building!

"And you can keep my apples sir, I don't really like them, but trust me, there really is only three of them!"

English, now these may seem strange words, from someone undertaking the challenge of writing a book.
Knowing if a word, is a verb, a noun, or an adjective, allow me to be honest here, to this day, even in the midst of this literary attempt, I'm never quite sure, I don't feel as though I've ever needed to know.

As I write this book, at no point yet, and I'll let you should that change at any point during the course, have I ever sat and thought;

"I know what this paragraph needs, really needs, what it's blatantly calling out for, is a witty, descriptive conjunction, or a clever little pronoun, maybe an adjective that will keep the reader hooked, I'm stuck for choice here, I really can't decide, should I go with a simile or a metaphor, in fact, I might even risk a cheeky little synonym!"

However, I have thought;

"What words sounds best here"

Now I know, if there any English teachers are out there, they will undoubtedly be in a position to rip this book and my writing skills, into tiny little shreds, quoting misuse of most of the commons laws of the English Language and Grammar, and maybe some that don't even exist yet.

I admit, I have failings, my grammatical prowess lacking, I mean, being honest, the only positive thing I can say about my Grammar;

> *"Is that she made the best Egg and Chips ever, and
> my Grandad will back me up on that!"*

Now Science, that was different, that has proved extremely useful on so many occasions in the course of my everyday life, I've lost count how many times, when faced with a particular problem, a difficult task, a dilemma of large proportion, that the solution lay, not in logic, not in a careful, measured approach, using the skills, that overcoming the toils associated with life, instils in us.

But with a trip down to the shed, where I would instinctively, take my trusty Bunsen burner, a strip of magnesium, and I would proceed to burn that magnesium, watching, in awe as it turned bright yellow in the flames.

Got me out of some very sticky situations that has! I can tell you!

Now, be honest, that was, in truth, probably, one of the better days of school life, that day, in the Science Lab, donning an apron and safety googles, playing with fire, it was fun, it held a sense of danger, and look at those pretty colours in the flame, and ooh that smell!

I still remember it now, but, what was the reason, what did we learn from that, what indeed, can be learned from that?

And that relates to a point made by Daniele over the last couple of years, during her time at school, she too, did the same science experiments, the same maths equations. There to, were missing apples, misplaced pronouns and the like, she was exposed to a plethora of information, facts and knowledge.

Which, is great, but, on leaving school, entering the big wide world, she was lacking in important skills.

Now faced with the complexities involved with, for example, securing a student loan to assist in her training, or the minefield of self-tax assessments, the challenge of dealing with invoices and the like, things like that were initially, a struggle, and she relied heavily on our help and support, which we happy, of course to offer, now this isn't an effort for me, to shirk my parental responsibilities.

I just feel, as did Danielle, that over the course of five years in a Secondary School Education, there could surely be more opportunity to learn about post school life, the real challenges that lie ahead, enabling that students leave equipped, yes with academic knowledge, exam results, but in tandem with a well-rounded knowledge that best prepares them for adult life and its real challenges.

But, as in most, professions, environments, in this generation, focus is solely, on targets, numbers, those exam pass rates, it matters not the individual and their ability to cope, it matters what marks they attain, judged not on actual ability, but on the grades that they achieve.

I think, looking back, the only subject I really enjoyed, looked forward to, was PE, I was competent in most sports, never that poor individual left standing alone at the end when picking teams.

Now, be honest, there is a certain ruthless inevitability surrounding that selection process;

"Everybody, line up, you two are the captains,
now take turns and pick your teams"

There is a natural order to this selection process, with best mates and the most skilled individuals chosen in the early part, moving down, methodically, through the array of average participants, before finally the remaining few, shall we say, the less well equipped, the pupils for whom sport was not a natural ability, the ones so blatantly lacking.

It must be so hurtful, soul-destroying, when standing there, feeling the numbers dwindle, as captain of each team, selects player after player, ahead of you, leaving you stood, finally, alone, *'the last one picked'*

A look of despair on the face of the captain, who has no other option left, but to take you, looking at him apologetically, safe in the knowledge that you have, just weakened his team with your presence.

One of our PE teachers, the old school type, on the brink of retirement when he sadly, suddenly passed, an event that shook the school at the time, sending shockwaves around the place, affecting both staff and students alike.

He was a popular teacher, inspirational.
He had a quote he would roll out at every opportunity, whenever anyone showed any, lack confidence, doubt, or indeed ability.

Inspiration indeed, for those poor individuals, last man standing, during those merciless team selections.

'Genius is 1% Inspiration, 99% Perspiration'

I liked that, and I think it rings very true, we all look at David Beckham, floating a free kick over a wall, into the top corner of the net, and we're all guilty, speaking of him, as a natural talent, born with such amazing skill.
In truth, 99% of the reason he can do that with a football can be attributed to the hours and hours of practice on the training ground practising those free kicks.

It reminds me of a story I once heard about, it was attributed to Gary Player, a professional golfer on the tour, although evidence suggests he did not actually coin the adage himself, in fact, in a book by himself, he attributed the aphorism to fellow golfer Jerry Barber.

In truth, it seems that the words, or different combinations of them, had been in use since well before the 1900s.

But for the purpose of this book, I will quote the story as told by Gary Player, in an interview published in Golf Monthly in 2002;

I was practicing in a bunker down in Texas and this
good old boy with a big hat stopped to watch.
The first shot he saw me hit went in the hole.
He said, "You got 50 bucks if you knock the next one in."
I holed the next one.
Then he says,
"You got $100 if you hole the next one."
In it went for three in a row.
As he peeled off the bills he said,
"Boy, I've never seen anyone so lucky in my life."
And I shot back,

"Well, the harder I practice, the luckier I get."

Now, in the same way that Gary Player probably wasn't the first person to use the adage, I wouldn't be so naive as to suggest it was my PE teacher that was the original author of that other quote, the inspiration/perspiration one.

Otherwise, he probably wouldn't have been my PE teacher, alternatively teaching Sociology or the like, at a big posh University somewhere.

But no, he was a PE teacher, at an average Secondary School, my school!
And he was the one who said it to me, so it is he, who I thank for those words of true inspiration.

A big difficulty I had to endure throughout my school life was following in the footsteps of my big sister, not only was she a top student, she was *'the'* top student, extremely clever, hardworking and committed, the perfect scholar, not only that, born at the beginning of the school year meant she was the oldest in the year.

Now I might have mentioned previously at some point, I'm not sure if you're aware, but I was the youngest in my year!

That resulted in, despite there being the best part of a two year age gap, we were actually in consecutive *'school'* years, so I had the pleasure of following her through each and every one of those long, arduous years.

Each new year, to be greeted with a teachers realisation of who I was, a common name like Smith, or Jones, would have kept me under the radar, but in a small town like Oswaldtwistle, a name like Corson was hardly going to go unnoticed;

> *"Ian Corson? ah, Debbie's brother, I presume, I taught her last year, excellent student, I look forward to teaching you to Ian"*

Don't Miss, please don't look forward to it, don't go getting your hopes up, I would hate to see you suffer the same grave disappointment of my previous teachers.

And so it would transpire, within weeks I would see that familiar look of total dismay across that teachers face, that sense of disillusionment, I could hear them thinking,

> *"He can't be, no way, a Corson? Debbie's brother, no, he must have been adopted or something!"*

And so, I stumbled, limped through school life, now all I had to contend with were those final GCSE's.

To be fair, to my credit I actually did alright in my mock exams, gaining respectable grades, grades that would ultimately, prove to be undoing, my GCSE downfall, for based on those mock grades I was offered an Engineering Apprenticeship, no small feat for a student who's metalwork teacher had concluded to my parents;

> *"I'll be honest with you, he's struggling"*

I'm struggling in metalwork, so the most natural progression, an apprenticeship in it, a job!

"Yeah, that makes perfect sense Ian, I'm sure you and your career are going to live a very long, fruitful and happy life together!"

My motivation for this strangest of decisions?
Well my dad was an engineer, and his company were offering apprenticeships, he had a word with the Personnel manager, and;

"Ian, how do you fancy a job?"

"Yeah, whatever, can I have egg and chips for tea first though!"

So having secured this opportunity prior to taking my actual GCSE exams, it kind of negated the need, in my mind at least, to give much effort towards them, after all, I didn't need them now, or so I thought.

Years later, when I was attending night school, at my own cost, in my own time, and with a full time job and a young family to contend with, I realised just how wrong, very wrong, I was.

I was in the process of a career change, yet due to my misjudgement of the importance of those exam qualifications back then, I now found myself a GCSE short for the application process.

Luckily, I had gained a slight semblance of success in Maths at school. Gaining a Grade 1, CSE pass, in the subject, equating, to a GCE pass, so despite my ineptitude, I had a least gained the two most important subjects.
English and Maths.

Now, for those of who might not know what a CSE is, it's basically a qualification similar, but lesser to, a GCE, a combination of the two, later in time, culminating in the more commonly known, GCSE.

I suspect that CSEs were created with the aim, that all students, would leave school with some form of exam qualification, even the most challenged students, if they spelt there name right on the exam paper, there you go, got yourself a Grade 3 CSE.

And luckily, in Maths, I had used my crayons to good effect, keeping in between the lines when colouring in, and not getting into any problematic debates regarding Derren Brown and his magic apples.

So, with all those family and work commitments in tow, I proceeded, to night school, enrolling for a course, GCSE Psychology.

Juggling family, work and my time as a mature student proved hard, but luckily I had chosen a subject, to which I fully engaged, Psychology.

I found it totally captivating, incredibly interesting, I developed a fascination for the material that was matched closely with my endeavour, I worked hard, contributed much to the in-depth discussions.

The tutor, a man who I considered to be the very best at his chosen art, I won't call him a teacher, in the main because, well he didn't actually teach, instead. He discussed, informed, with relative anecdotes that would add sound and colour to the material, stories that would flavour those words, making them palatable.

It was the easiest I have ever found learning, it just goes to show, the right tutor and the right subject teamed with a student with the right attitude,

I not only passed, I did so gaining an A* pass.

I was so impressed with myself, it seemed I had more ability, than I ever thought I had, and on the day I had to go and collect my result, alongside all those teenagers collecting theirs, I was filled with a deep, warming, sense of achievement.

By now, it should come as no great surprise to you all, to learn that Danielle accompanied me on that trip to the college to pick up my results.

The day she, infamously (you need to watch a certain video clip on YouTube to fully understand this) spoke the words;

"I'm Danielle Corson, I love my daddy!"
"And you know what, today, he got his report, and it says"
"A, well actually, A star"
"He's a star is my dad!"

It became a popular video within the circle of our friends and family, and when Danielle chose Psychology, plans were afoot to re-create that video, once she too, had gained an A*in the subject.

I was to film myself, in much the way she had, using that same script;

"I'm Ian Corson, I love my daughter!"
"And you know what, today, she got her report, and it says"
"A, well actually, A star"
She's a star is my daughter!"

As with any great plan, there was a flaw, there always is, she passed, and with a good mark, but sadly just short of enough to gain an A*, and with that, the opportunity for the video to be filmed, and then most likely go viral, was scuppered.

But it enhanced my achievement, Danielle is a very clever girl, far more so than I am, so for me to out achieve her, it spoke volumes regarding my effort.

If only I had known how good success like that felt, all those years ago, when I sat those original exams, then maybe, just maybe I would have worked that little bit harder.

On one occasion, leading up to those big exams, those GCE's, we'd been given the opportunity to bypass the normal timetable and choose whatever we wanted to do, to give time to any subject we felt would benefit us,
If it was maths, yeah I know very unlikely, I could just pop down to the maths department and spend some valuable time with Derren Brown and his magic apples.

It was an access all areas opportunity.

Following huge deliberations, me and my mate, John settled for a morning in the gym playing football, followed by a pint in the pub around the corner.

So with very little surprise, my GCSE results left much to be desired, as I say, in life, you get out, exactly what you put in.

And so, I started on my apprenticeship journey.

For four years I studied my craft, I drilled, I sawed, I filed, I bolted things together, hit things with hammers, and to be honest, it wasn't all bad, I quite enjoyed it, not the work, that I found as interesting and futile as I did a maths equation.

But the ambience, the workplace, the banter, I loved that.

So for four years I honed my real craft, my humour.
An engineering workshop is an environment filled with an abundance of banter, craic and humour, wind ups, jokes.
I revelled in it, and as an apprentice I was learning from some of the best.

But it wasn't enough, I'd developed an urge to travel, it made sense to stay and finish my apprenticeship, I'd always have it then, as a backup, it might even lend itself to another job, I considered pipe fitting, I'd enjoyed my time spent working in that department, I looked into jobs on the oil rigs, they paid well and they would open up travel opportunities.

Yeah, travelling to the middle of a desolate ocean!

*"Good plan Ian, go strand yourself on a big steel island,
and see the world!"*

Ok, admittedly, my plans required a little tweak here and there.

Another option I gave consideration to, was that, I had relatives in Australia, well Tasmania to be accurate, maybe I could go stay with them, find work, putting up fencing or something.

The point was, I was young, I had no commitments and the world is a big and interesting place.

Enter fate, as I approached the end of my training a position became available in our customer services department for a Service Engineer Technician, travelling that said world installing and servicing our machinery.

Given that I had, the last two years running been awarded Apprentice of the Year, not only for my company, but for the town of Blackburn and its surrounding area.

Incredible I know, lil ole me, Mr egg and chips, Mr struggling in metalwork.

I can only assume that the standard in those two years was particularly poor, but won them I had.
So with confidence brimming, I threw my hat into the ring, I applied for the position, and luckily, I was successful.

I got the job, and I spent the next few years travelling around the world, and getting paid for it.
What would my metalwork teacher have made of all that I wonder.

Whilst most of that time was spent in Europe, there were times spent in more interesting places, China, America, South Africa, places that offered so much more in experiences.

On a trip to Pakistan, I flew to Islamabad airport, before undertaking a three hour car journey across the country, passing through little villages; I sat there transfixed by the visions playing out in front of me.

For four weeks, despite, living in relative squalor, my accommodation basic, no more than an office at the factory, with a bed in the corner, and very little else.

I was blessed to be able to share the culture, the food, the people and the views, from the vantage point of the factory roof I was surrounded by the most amazing views of the Afghanistan mountains, a perfect time and place for true contemplation.

They say that travel broadens the mind, and it does, it really does, that period in my life was defining, it gave me a lot of the beliefs I hold today, it gave me a lot of understanding.

It improved me as a person, and I certainly would recommend it, in fact it's something I have always preached to Danielle and Ben,

Indeed, I say to you all;

"It's a big world out there, go visit it, see it, experience all those different cultures, speak those different languages, if only to say nothing more than please and thank you, go eat that food, hear their music, go and learn, embrace the vastness of this land and sea"

It was during my time travelling that I discovered I enjoyed reading, you see, a lot of the time I travelled alone, which meant, I had to drink and eat alone, now I'll be honest, I'm an avid people watcher, I can easily keep myself entertained in a bar or restaurant just looking around the room, watching people and their many interesting quirks.

But it's nice to have a backup, and back then that was a book.

Today, in these modern times it's a mobile phone that has become the backup, it's a comforter, a dummy, a pacifier, something we can reach for at times when we feel a little uncomfortable, aware of our solitude in an environment.

Be honest, how many times have you picked your phone up for no another reason than to avoid that uncomfortable, awkward feeling when sat alone in a bar, or on a train or a bus stop.

But as it turned out, I actually enjoyed it, I stumbled across one particular author, whose books I found interesting, funny and altogether very enjoyable reads.

His name, Bill Bryson, a very funny travel writer.

I would highly recommend his work.

Go find yourself a copy of 'A Walk in the Woods' it's absolutely brilliant, highly informative and, at times, hilarious.

It transpires, that it recently made the crossover from book, onto the silver screen, made into a full length movie, with the famous actors Robert Redford and Nick Nolte, accurately por-traying the characters of Bill and his trusted friend Katz.
It proved a successful movie, but in my humble opinion, I would suggest the book is better, so go find it people, read it.

On reflection, I should probably charge him some form of com-mission, for promoting him in this book, blatantly plugging his material, who knows, maybe he will return the compliment in his next literary outing.

> "Come on Billy boy, don't be shy, come give
> lil ole me a bit of a mention"

Now travelling, as fun and interesting as it is, isn't particularly conducive to marriage and children, so when it came to that stage of my life I gave up that job, I stayed at the same company, but in my 30s I felt I had grown as a person, now ready to take a decision on what to do with my career, I didn't foresee a big future for engineering generally.

And a future with me in it seemed even less appealing.

So I looked around, and found something that appealed to me.
I spent the next few years working towards it and then, at the age of 38, I hung up my hammer, I left the company I had spent the last 24 years at, and my career took the most radical of changes.

Joining the Ambulance Service as an Emergency Medical Technician, a position I have held for the last twelve years, and indeed, still hold today.

It has to be one of the biggest challenges I have ever taken, and as you're aware, there's been a couple, that bloody cd button, and those forays onto the stage.
But this was massive, life changing, I was leaving the security of a job with decent pay, at a company I had been employed by since leaving school, that provided a twenty four year comfort blanket, and I was leaving a job that, having done so long, held little in being problematic.

And I was moving, not just to another company, but to an organisation, a big one at that, to a job requiring new skills, with new challenges, in an unfamiliar environment and with new colleagues.

As part of my background to this venture, in the early days of giving consideration to a potential career change, I had undertaken work, in a voluntary capacity, at Burnley General Hospital, on a Medical Elective Ward.

There, I would make cups of tea, serve meals, make-up beds, pretty much whatever needed doing, at that given time, within my capabilities.
But the biggest part of that role came with my interaction with the patients.

The reason for this voluntary position was two-fold, it provided experience within a patient background that would benefit my application in the recruitment process, and secondly, it allowed me to spend time in that patient environment, I could dip a toe in the water, see if I really did want to jump, dive-bomb, into the depths of that new career.

It handed me that time, time that the nursing staff didn't have, due to their ever-increasing, already heavy workload, time to just sit, and chat.
Being an elective ward, the majority of those patients were the elderly.
I would sit, often denied the opportunity to offer much towards the conversation, except to listen, to just sit and listen.

I hold a strong belief, that every person, whoever they may be, has an interesting story to tell, and everyone's story is different, interesting and individually unique to that person.

Sadly, as was the case with these patients in their later years, there isn't always someone to listen to those stories, a fact I find incredibly sad.
During my time there, I handed that opportunity to them, an opportunity they seized upon with vigour.

The experience enhanced my endeavour, it strengthened my resolve to undertake this most dramatic of career changes. I enjoyed the patient environment, and it proved, not only to my prospective employers, but more importantly, to myself, that I was more than comfortable within that environment.

The application and recruitment process was swift, within two weeks from my application, I had attended Isometric testing, completed a driving evaluation, endured a rigorous fitness test, and finally, the last stage, attended an Interview, sat before a panel.

I was asked during that interview, what trait I would most like to find in my crew-mate, my colleague, now had I been given time to sit and think, logically, I suspect my response would have been *'empathy'*

Yeah, that seemed like the most measured response.

But, it was an interview, I didn't have time to sit and think, I was busy sweating and shaking, that was always my interview technique
I blurted out the most instinctive of answers, the most honest;

"A sense of humour"

I sat there aghast with my response, pondering;

*"Are you thick, stupid, you just given the panel the idea
that the person who is your ideal mate, is someone
you can piss about with, having a good laugh"*

The head of the panel, interjected, interrupting my thoughts, my self-chastising thoughts;

*"Excellent answer, the perfect answer actually, I'll tell you now, if you
don't have a good sense of humour when you join the Ambulance
Service, by hell you'll have a good one by the time you leave"*

This was good, not only had the crisis been averted, it seemed I had found someone I'd quite like to work a shift with, it seemed like he was up for pissing about a lot too!

I was fortunate enough to be offered the position, and in June 2007, with more than a little apprehension, I started the twelve week training course, alongside eleven other fresh recruits.

The course consisting of three weeks of driving, learning to drive safely, on blue lights, followed by twelve weeks of Anatomy and Physiology.

The entire twelve weeks became an intense, long hard slog, I was tested to my limit, not everyone who started that course, made it to the end to complete it, giving testament to its demanding, arduous and at times, soul destroying, nature.

In truth, most of the learning really starts on competition of the course, during that first, initial probationary year, you learn with experience, hands-on experience, and whilst it was, at times, extremely nerve wracking and daunting, it is done, within the confines of a group of colleagues, who have taken that road before you, they understand what it's like, and they are there to offer, support, advice and encouragement.

It's a job, in which you never stop learning, every shift a school day, the diversity of the role means, you will never have experienced everything, and the diversity of the role means there is always an incident, lurking around the corner, ready to test your skills and resolve.

Initially, you are based as reserve staff, as cover, you work at a number of different stations, with different people, working different shifts.

Once established, in time, you work up that ladder, and are granted a permanent shift line, working a dedicated shift pattern, with a regular crew-mate from a single station.

It is at this time I should introduce you to my work-wife, Mark, my crew mate for the last nine years, now I have to say, the teaming up of crews can be a little bit of a lottery.

It's like having a box of chocolates, but fate dictates which chocolate you're handed from the box, no-one wants lumbering with the Turkish delight, or the sticky caramel one that instantly welds itself to the back of your teeth.

And when that time came, the time to get my chocolate, I was lucky, very lucky, I was given the perfect one; solid on the inside, yet soft in the right places, sweet but not sickly, but most importantly, totally nutty!

We are so matched in our sense of humour, yeah he pisses about a lot too, resulting in moments of pure hilarity, albeit in a private-joke kind of way, there is an edge to ambulance staff humour that is individual to us, I suspect a coping mechanism, it's, not a humour that people outside of the environment might necessarily understand, but, as they say, if you don't laugh, you'll cry.

The amount of times, whilst recounting a story to someone out of the circle, whilst detailing the hilarity in fits of laughter, you look up to see a blank face, frowning, sometimes accompanied with a shake of the head, knowing that all they are thinking, is, what's wrong with this lunatic!

I suggest, if that sounds like your reaction, please, never, ever sit in a station mess room, when filled with a number of crews, it's not a place for you!

Aside from our sense of humour, we have much more in common, our values, our thoughts on how patients should be treated, we work well as a team. Highlighted by the comments of one family member of a patient we had on the back of the Ambulance.
We were busy doing everything that we needed to do, blood pressures, cannulation, drawing up drugs, morphine, anti-emetics, fluid therapy, a saline drip, ECG.

And, unnoticed by us, we had done all that with little communication between us, the family member had picked up on it;

> "You two must have worked together for a very long time, you've just done all that, and hardly spoke, it just happened, it was amazing to watch, like a well-oiled machine, I'm impressed"

We used to refer to ourselves as the oldest crew in the North West Ambulance Service, but as time passes, that has progressed to our introduction of;

> "You know, you're lucky to get us, we are the oldest crew, in the Northern Hemisphere"

And so, in what feels like a blink of an eye, I fast approach my thirteenth year, and Mark, well he's 60 this year, and intends to retire soon.

Now let me answer all your questions, I'm used to it, I get them
every single shift;

"Half six, I finish at half six"
"Half six, I started at half six"
"Yeah, 12 hours, it is a long time"
"Yeah, it has been busy, it always is"
"Yes, I do see some sights, and that's just the staff"

"12 years, that's how long I've been doing it"

*"Yes, we do have to queue up on this corridor waiting to be seen,
yes, you're right it's wrong, by the way, how is your mothers sore
toe right now, the one that's been sore for three months, that you've
decided at three o clock in the morning requires a visit to A&E ?"*

*"The worst job I've ever done? To be honest I'd rather not say,
what you're actually asking me to do is revisit, remember,
and recall a traumatic memory, one that I'd rather not, for the
sole purpose of nothing more than your entertainment"*

*"And finally, yes, we do have a warped sense of humour
and yes we do end up very cynical indeed!"*

And the big, probably most frequently asked;

"Do you love your job?"

Well, to be honest, not really, now don't get me wrong, it's actually a really good job, and I consider myself fortunate to do it,
but six numbers on the lottery this Saturday, and I'm off!

It's a job I like, that I enjoy, in the most part, but that is just what
it is, I have to work, to pay the bills, and its serves its purpose in

that fact.

I feel that I am fast approaching the stage in my life, where work is an unwanted attraction, an interference that keeps me away from the things I'd prefer to be doing.

I have worked, without a break in employment for the last thirty-five years, straight from leaving school, in the current climate; I consider that quite an achievement.
Now given that, during a lot of those years, it would include a lot of overtime hours being worked, in real terms, the result of which probably means I've worked well in excess of those thirty-five years.

I'm ready to try new challenges, this book, one of those.
I want to lean on my experience of music and dance, and create a production show.

I want to re-take up Golf.
Go for long walks with Pam.

As I say, it feels like work impedes on those aspirations, I suspect it's just a case of me getting older, edging ever closer to my retirement age of eighty-five (did I mention I worked for the NHS) and unless something radical occurs, like this book giving birth to a new career, yes, that would work, a full-time write, oh, I notice you're shaking your head apologetically, that's not going to happen is it.

Well, it's not all bad, I suppose.

I mean, I have some great shifts, I have some not so great shifts.
I meet some very lovely people, and some not quite so nice.

At times, I feel privileged, to meet who I meet, to see what I see, people open their doors to you, welcome you into their house, be it a mansion or a place that you wipe your feet on the way out, not the way in.

They share the most intimate of details with you, trust you unconditionally, it really is a privilege at times.

It's something that me and Mark regularly say;

"We truly are very privileged"

The biggest problem, the massive downside, is how busy it is, every shift leaving you battered, drained, exhausted!

The constant pressures we're placed under, every minute of every shift scrutinised, squeezed, to try and get that little bit more.

I do my job to the best of my ability, because I want to, because I choose to, because I want to do it right. And that's how everyone should carry out their job.

In my position I see first-hand how certain jobs are on the increase, mental health, suicide, and homeless people.

That suggests to me, that somewhere, there are people, out there, in important positions within the country, well paid people, that put simply, just aren't doing their jobs right.

"So there you have it Confucius,
my old trusted friend"

"I chose a job I don't love, and therefore, I have
to work every single day of it"

CHAPTER 7 – DANCE SCHOOL

'Behind every dancer who believes in themselves, is a teacher who believed in them first'

I can remember, as a child, being taken on days out to the seaside, the car journey filled with an excited anticipation of the impending fun-filled excursion. A customary game onroute of;

"First to spot Blackpool Tower can have an ice-cream when we get there"

Resulting, as always, in everybody getting an ice cream when we got there, but we never let that detract from our eagerness to be the first to see it, eyes scanning the horizon impatiently, screaming out at the mere glimpse of an electric pylon in the distance, a fierce determination to be the eagle-eyed victor, the winner, the champion.

It was usually my dad, which is no real surprise, given the fact that he was the inventor of the game, it's true, he was, all dads lay claim to that, and I know, because I invented it myself a few years later.

I enjoyed that game, it was always fun, yes for the most part it was a mere ploy, a tactic, to detract away from our endless requests of;

"Are we there yet?"

But it made the journey palatable, and much more enjoyable.

Now, all these years later, I'm in the car, taking my own family on that journey to Blackpool, but the mood in the car is different, it's quiet, there is an air of apprehension, and there is no game.

The reason for this journey is not for a fun-filled, care-free, family day out; this is the day we are taking Danielle to Dance College, on the next step of her journey. We will be dropping her off at her accommodation, where she will meet up with her new, fellow students, and we will make the journey home, without her.

The Little Acorn, continuing to grow, was spreading its branches just a little further.

I could sense, and understand, how daunting this would feel for her, just as it had done all those years ago when she attended her first ever dance class.

Danielle was nine when she announced, that she, along with her best friend Liv, wanted to go to dance lessons.

The local amateur dramatic company, Accrington Amateurs, had, at that time a junior company, called Buddies. My nephew Ross had performed with them, so it made perfect sense to approach them in the first instance, Danielle and Liv joined up, and started dancing.

The girl entrusted with teaching them and choreographing the show routines, Katie, had in the previous few months, created and started her own little dance school, Ktz Dance.

Quite innovative that, she's called Katie, so *'Kay-tees Dance'.* Now you think that that was fairly self-explanatory, but the number of times at a Competition they would be introduced as *'Kay-Tee-Zed Dance'*, it would invariably lead to a roll of the eyes from Katie and a look of total dismay.

It's motto; *'Dance for Fun'*, it was to offer an informal, friendly, inclusive, environment, to learn, to dance, but to have fun doing it.

With a handful of students, and the renting of an old church hall for an hour on Friday evenings, it seemed the logical next step for Danielle and Liv.

And so it started, Danielle's journey had begun, although at that time, we couldn't envisage the full nature of that journey, where it might lead, and the amazing experiences and opportunities that lay along its path.

A few months later, her first show, at a local golf club with no stage, they danced their routines, on a tiny floored area, it was humble beginnings, for both Danielle and the dance school, but it was the beginning of a relationship that was to flourish, hand in hand, their development interwoven, they would both develop, grow, together.

Things advanced quickly, as the school progressed, so too did Danielle, undertaking more lessons, private lessons, taking on more types of dance. Bigger, more suitable premises were found, the number of students on the increase, the shows becoming bigger, at more suitable venues.

In those early days, as a newcomer to dance, and not having any appreciation of the finer points of the art, many of those routines were wasted on me. As could be expected, if Danielle was involved in the routine, I was intently focussed. The catchy, upbeat numbers, I enjoyed those, they would keep my attention, sat there with feet tapping to the beat, the music made them enjoyable, see people, the music is important!

But those slow, what I called 'floaty' dances, I would become bored; find them a little tedious, mundane.

Ironically, once I had grasped 'dance', once the penny had dropped, Lyrical would become one of my favourite sections, it holds such potential for emotive expression, as technically impressive as an Arabesque, or a Grand Jette may be, it's those little things, the subtle movements, that show of emotion, those are what can create that shiver down your spine, and lyrical lends itself well to those moments.

A simple pause, doing absolutely nothing at all, can be the highlight, the most powerful part of a routine. But only, of course, if it's intended, not those paused moments when the dancer has simply forgotten the routine, their mind a total blank. If you're a dancer, you're able to relate, to understand, because if you're a dancer, you've been there, everyone has as some point, it must be terrifying, and the enormity of the situation will depend largely on your reaction.

The options being, you stand there, completely frozen, before retreating, running off stage with tears streaming, or you will gather your composure and thoughts together quickly, and just basically blag it, improvise, do whatever you can to complete the routine, in as dignified a manner as possible.

I suspect, if it was me, standing there, frozen on stage, well, I would choose option C....throwing myself to the floor, fake a seizure, or maybe even death, keeping the act up until my sorry corpse was dragged off to the sanctity of backstage.

I really do think those humble beginning had a positive effect on Danielle, this wasn't a big fancy, established school, where you turn up and everything is on hand, she witnessed the struggles, she experienced the hard work that went on around the school, it was a good grounding, it gave a perspective, a value, a meaning. It lead to an appreciation, an understanding, it was inspirational.

The school had flirted with an informal, local dance competition, which had proven highly successful, especially for such a small school in its first competitive outing.

They won a good number of trophies that day, and with that, the decision was taken; that the school would adopt a Competition team within the school, catered for by additional lessons, for students that wanted to make the progression to that stage, to compete at Dance Festivals.

I witnessed all the hard work, the attention to detail, the hours of practice undertaken, in preparation for that inaugural Festival.

Over the course of that weekend, I watched, and I learnt so much, as did Danielle, as did the school as a whole.

Success can be measured in many different ways, at the end of that festival; there were no trophies, no winning, but was there was, was a new found knowledge, there was experience, the school and Danielle knew where they were, and more importantly, where they needed to be.

The festival had given them insight, it had set the bar, and set it high, but the important thing, that they took from that festival, what made it a success, was what was that they left that festival with, a plan, a challenge, to work hard and reach up to that bar.

As a little aside, I have to mention, over the course of that weekend, the school was met with episodes of derision from some, not all, of the other, bigger, more established schools. it filled me with disgust, yes, we were a small school, new to the 'circuit', yes we were a little 'green' in areas, but what we were not, was deserving of sneering comments, ridicule and mockery. Whilst I agree, it is a competitive environment, schools and students are there, striving to be the best, to gain success, but there is no room for snobbery or contempt.

I suggest, if you're stood high up that festival ladder, and glance back to see a new school, a small school, don't look down on them with disdain, reach down, and offer a helping hand. For despite competing against each other, ultimately we are all here for the same reason, a common denominator, which is, a love of dance.

The experience instilled a little fight in the school, that at the next festival, we would not be new, it would not be our first time, we would not be so 'green' as on that first occasion.

And so, there was a plan; more lessons, more rehearsals, more commitment, better costumes, Ian was banging on about better music, as usual, something about not liking Mondays!

Now of course, all those additional lessons, rehearsals, they all incurred additional costs, and as any parent of a child that attends a dance school will know, they can soon mount up, spiral almost out of control. As I said at the very beginning, dance is an expensive hobby. I've been asked on many occasions, by different people;

"Is all that money spent on dance really worth it?"

Allow me to explain;

'Cost is what you pay, value is what you get'

In a way, cost is what we paid, and value is what Danielle got, and that value goes well beyond any dance moves that she might have acquired, you see, with dance comes so much more. Dance requires discipline, it teaches it and it demands it, it leads to a controlled level of self-discipline that will lend itself to every element of life.

Dance teaches commitment, in abundance, a frozen December night spent in a bitter cold dance studio, whilst your friends are busy attending Christmas parties. Dance teaches motivation, it's what drags your weary body to that studio on that December night when you're full of a cold.

Dance teaches teamwork, the sense of achievement it brings with the realisation that you are an important cog in that finely tuned piece of machinery that is a well performed, group routine.

Dance teaches autonomy, self-determination, it will serve you well when you take up your starting position for that big solo routine. Dance teaches achievement and belief, the feeling that overwhelms you on leaving that stage at the end of that solo.

Danielle has taken all that she learnt from dance, and is taking those skills with her on her journey as a professional dancer, but what of her friends, the dancers that attended the dance school, that gained those same skills, but have taken an alternate career path.

Those skills will be still prove priceless, whatever that career path may be, because Dance teaches more, infinitely more than steps, movement, routines; it teaches all the qualities that are an integral part of life itself.

So what about the benefactors, those poor parents parting with their hard earned money, what do they get out of it?

Primarily, that immense feeling of pride that comes from watching your daughter performing, seeing her gain success, experiencing alongside her those highs, but there is much more to it. Knowing she has gained all those qualities I've just spoken about, knowing that she has matured into an adult, with the right values, the best qualities and a good solid foundation, that will serve her well in her future.

We watched Danielle as she went through her teenage years, that time of adolescence, there were no problems, no drama, she didn't have time, she was busy, focussed, her time spent at the studio, not on a street corner, bored, frustrated with life, a recipe that can so often lead to a teenager choosing the wrong path and making wrong decisions. We never had that worry, those concerns that must haunt some parents, dance took them away.

Yes, admittedly, it is expensive, I have on many occasions, listened to other parents, bemoaning the fact of rising costs, how it is becoming a struggle, and later that night, that post on social media, the excitement on having just booked their third holiday of the year, and how they will celebrate that night with a meal at Pizza Express.

I guess the point is this; money, cost, value, it's all relative, and we all have our unique things that we deem worthy of spending our hard earned on, to some it will be clothing, so some cars, the list will be endless, but whatever it is, you will indeed spend that money, ultimately, because it will give you pleasure, joy, happiness.

So let me turn the question around, to you;

> "Is all that money spent on dance really worth it?"

We explained to Danielle, very early, that whatever commitment, endeavour, and hard work she invested into dance; we would contribute financially to the same degree, and that is what we have done.

Now I'll be honest, the money side of things, that's really not my department, not being at all financially astute, it was Pam who took control of that side of the operation, and let me tell you she did the most amazing of jobs with it. She was the one that, when we needed what wasn't there, she went out and found it, there were many occasions when she would hold Peter up at gunpoint, before taking her ill-gotten gains to Paul, now anyone not aware of the 'robbing Peter, to pay Paul', saying, I should clarify, Pam wasn't actually an armed robber, she didn't wander the streets holding passers-by up at gunpoint, although at times, it was an option that we kept in mind, just in case.

At times, things got tough, especially during the college years, compounded by the fact that, as she was attending a private college, she was not liable for any student funding. She didn't qualify for any student loan schemes or grants to help with accommodation, or costs of living away from home. We had to pay for everything, but it was our choice, we believed this college was the best, the most appropriate, so we took it on the chin. Pam, it has to be said worked miracles juggling our finances around, we couldn't have managed it without her, as for me, well, I'm stuck with writing a bloody book to pay off all the debt!

And so, it transpired, the plan worked, the additional lessons, the extra rehearsals, it was all paying off, with the next few competitions/festivals came success, initially on a small scale, but growing, quickly, each outing improved upon in the following one, the school was on an upward slope, and it was picking up speed.

Schools rely heavily on the involvement and the help of parents at these events, people who can be on hand to help with make-up, costume changes, someone fool hardy enough to sit and press play on the cd player, don't worry, there's always someone thick enough to fall for it!

Schools need these volunteers, prepared to sacrifice an entire weekend, not to just help their own child, but all the children competing that day, and they are there to support all those students on the day, not just their own.

It has to be said, it will always be the same faces you will see, every competition, the same parents will be there, and it is the same parents that will appear, fleetingly, a guest appearance almost, to watch their own child's performance, before leaving as abruptly as they had arrived, which is fine, understandable, there were times when that is what Pam had to do, I get it.

What cause annoyance, frustration, was that, ironically, it was those parents who were the most vocal on the schools shortcomings, who had the most to say about how the school was failing their child in those competitions, their child, that was now sat at home, while her their fellow students were still performing, missing out on the opportunity to learn, improve from watching other dancers, other routines, but, on the bright side, they'd be getting Pizza Express for tea!

It was at one of those festivals where Danielle pointed out an old man, possibly in his seventies, he was there, every single day, in the same seat, ready for the very first dance of the day, not leaving until after the final routine of the day. Danielle found him adorable, so cute, that he would sit, intently watching, enjoying each and every dance.

He sat, in that seat, even though the lunch-break, reaching down into his bag, retrieving his tin-foiled wrapped sandwiches, pouring a hot drink from his flask, I didn't even see him leave his seat to visit the toilets, I'm guessing he must have been catheterised, either that, or someone had a big job washing down his seat at the end of the festival.

Me and Danielle pondered about him, what his history was, there had to be one, was his late wife a principal, a teacher, a dance, was it him, did he used to grace to boards in his day, was it his family, we imagined many reasons, even those that involved him signing a register on occasion.

In hindsight, I was a little sad I didn't introduce myself to him, learn his story, I suspect he would have enjoyed sharing it. It was with a smile that Danielle nudged me at one point during a break, nodding over to him;

> *"That's you dad, that's you in the future, when I'm off somewhere, dancing abroad, you'll be here, sat in your own little chair, watching the dances, getting your fix."*

As I've said before;

> *'Many a true work, spoken in jest'*

It's true, I had grown to love dance, understand it, I might not be aware of the finer complexities of the techniques, but do I have, in my opinion, and understanding, that enables me to differentiate between something that looks good, and something that doesn't.

I used to enjoy the game, during those festivals, predicting the winners, first, second and third place, and in truth, I think I held my own. It was on one of those occasions, that the realisation hit me, that dance had got me hooked, it had got under my skin, it will do that if you let it.

I was deliberating on the Ballet section, pondering on whom I deemed the best. I was suddenly hit with what I was doing, ballet?

What happened to football Ian, how did this happen, trading the atmosphere and excitement of the big match for a pair of pointe shoes!

Well, let me tell you something here, I bought tickets to the ballet for me and Danielle, my thinking was that it would possibly keep my interest for a little while, but Danielle would love it. And so we took our seats, by the time the interval arrived, I had enjoyed it and was looking forward to the second half, by the end of the show, I was giving a standing ovation, clapping vigorously, it was an amazing experience, for me, Danielle's opinion less vociferous, whilst she had enjoyed it, it was probably a little too classical for her.

Imagine, lil ole me, a night at the ballet, I would never have envisaged that, not in a million years, only that, I now had a favourite ballet dancer. At work once, on lunch break, I was watching on YouTube, a video documenting the background to this said dancer, the lad I was working with could overhear, and questioned what I was watching, when I told him, his face adopted a look of total bewilderment, "You, ballet?"… and that kind of sums it up, yes, I like ballet, specifically Contemporary Ballet, I had stumbled across a video of this dancer, I expect you've probably seen it, as it was splashed all over social media at the time, he is called Sergei Polunin, a Ukrainian, who became the Royal Ballets youngest ever Principal dance at the age of just twenty. The video is a contemporary ballet dance to Hozier's 2013 hit, *'Take Me To Chuch'*, if you haven't already seen it, I fully recommend it, it truly is something special.

Danielle started dancing at another school, which was more 'street' orientated, at that time it wasn't readily catered for at Ktz, and her friend Georgia wanted to start dancing again, so together they attended the other one, RM House of Fusion, based in Accrington.

We didn't realise at the time, but it's not really considered appropriate to be involved with more than one school at a time, in fact, some schools actually forbid it, but in truth, it was good for Danielle, as they both offered different things, and that opened up more opportunities to her.

Street competitions being much more, relaxed, fun, informal events in comparison with a traditional Dance Festivals, benefitted Danielle in many ways, and her street technique improved under the guidance of Razia, the experiences and opportunities she offered enhanced Danielle's performance level too, many people played their part in her progression, and Razia is one of those, and I will always be grateful for the time she spent with her.

Georgia, her friend was very close to us as a family, spending much time in our company, pretty much becoming a part of our family really, joining us on holiday a number of times, we don't see as much of her these days, she has a fulltime career, taking exams to qualify her, standing on her own two feet, she lives on her own, and I am immensely proud of all her achievements.

Ktz Dance had been given an opportunity to attend a competition in Disneyland Paris, it offered so much, and I don't mean just those amazing dancing dads!

The effort and hard work that went into the preparations for that competition was phenomenal, a credit to Katie and everyone involved with the school, every small detail was catered for, the organisation was faultless, to ensure not only a successful outcome in terms of routines, but also the tiny matter of not just getting all those children safely over there, but also getting them all back, parents can be a bit touchy about losing a child to a school trip. The whole event proved a major success, and it reaped its rewards with a huge collection of trophies, and more importantly a group of students that had the most amazing experience.

An experience that was to be repeated on a further two occasions, the last one whilst Danielle was studying at college, the trip had come at a time that clashed with rehearsals for the college show, so to enable her to do both, she would fly back from Paris, on her own a day early, quite an undertaking really. I recall her ringing me from the hotel as she was waiting for the taxi to pick her up to take her to the airport, she asked;

"The car that's picking me up, do you think it will be a man driving"

Now, I soon picked up on the vibes, that she was possibly a little wary, a car journey with a stranger, in a foreign country, on her own, I set about putting her mind at ease immediately;

"Well, it was in the film Taken"

"Now don't forget to give me a quick ring from under the bed"

I know what you're all thinking now, yes, my parenting skills would benefit from a little tweak here and there at times. But hey, I allowed her to go dance in Disney three times, so I'm not all bad!

Its little surprise I get some of the most amazing Father's Day presents really, one of which one year, was tickets for the two of us, for an immersive dance production, in all honesty that's about as much as we knew about it, until we went.

It was fantastically good, the 'show' began when we boarded a bus in Blackburn Town Centre, not your typically average 'show' experience this, and I liked that, I like different, this was in no way a traditional show, and you know me!

Unknowingly to us, most of the cast were in the queue, and had boarded the bus alongside us, the audience.

What followed was a show of pure genius, such an innovative concept, and choreographed mayhem ensued with the characters, as we went on our bus journey, driving around the town, whilst being blessed with little impromptu encounters with the characters.

We would make scheduled stops around the town, where scenes were pre-set, ready for the next stage of the performance.

The show was, as you'd expect highly interactive and at one of those stops, I was given my opportunity to shine, as they worked through the group, I could sense that moment was close.

I hoped my task would be an easy one, and then I got flashback, to that time trying to walk in time to music, back in the days of the dancing dads, that hadn't gone well, not well at all, chances were slim that this was going to get any easier than just walking.

But I didn't worry, due in fact, to not having time to, she was already pointing at me.

My task was simple, it was to copy her, just repeat her moves, I was hoping for a little shimmy or something along those lines.

So when I saw her throw herself forward, into a handstand, it didn't instil a great deal of confidence in me.

I mean, the last time, in fact, every time, I had previously done a handstand, and those times weren't all that often it reality, it had been against a wall, here there was no wall.

I could have happily punched her in the throat at the next bit, walking forward on her hands, she was good, she made it look easy, and so she should with, I presume, three years of dance and performing arts under her belt.

I looked under my belt, all I could find was a pair of legs, and they had just started shaking.

I could feel a buzz of excitement, anticipation, building around the group, I looked at Danielle for inspiration, she was biting her lip, trying not to laugh, this did not bode well.

I resigned myself to the fact that this might not end in great success, but I thought, what the hell, just do it, go for it.

I threw myself forward, conscious, it transpired a little too conscious, of not going too far, over-cooking it and falling all the way over, crashing down onto my back.

I'd surveyed the landscape, and I was pretty sure there was nowhere suitable for the air ambulance to land anyway, and I've never really suited the attire of neck collar and spinal board.

So doing my handstand, with my legs pointing at about 90 degrees instead of point straight up at 180, I looked like I was attempting a 'wheelbarrow', but minus a partner.

I was never going to achieving walking forward on my hands, but try it I did. What I, in fact, achieved, as I lifted one hand in an attempt, and with more entertainment value that walking on my hands would have done.

Was the most dramatic, sudden, highly artistic….face plant!

It looked like I'd been shot, I went down like a sack of spuds, luckily my face broke my fall, I noticed the dancer running over, with deep concern engrained in her expression.

It worried me, what damage had I done?

Luckily it was minimal, superficial, with x rays later confirming that I had fractured my pride in six places, with a further three breaks in my self-esteem.

I glanced over at Danielle, I've never seen someone that worried, concerned yet still manage to cry in fits of laughter, it was good of her to put such a brave face on the situation.

And later, at the end of the performance, when the bus dropped us off, I looked back on it all, and even with my little mishap, it had been a truly memorable, amazing experience, the characters had put on the most fantastic show for us, and another positive, I was beginning to get the feeling back in my nose!

❖ ❖ ❖

Katie had given Danielle the opportunity, to help with teaching the younger children on Saturday mornings, it gave her a little pocket money, and the experience was beneficial to her, it was another step on her development path, and she adopted the role well, I enjoyed watching her, she was strict, I suppose you have to be with children that age, but she was fair and she taught them well. She had been given an opportunity, and as always, had grasped it with two hands.

It would be impossible to list all the opportunities that Katie presented to Danielle over the years, it was that kind of dance school, and she was fortunate to have spent her formative dance years there, Katie went above and beyond the duties of a principal/teacher, and the part that she and her school played in Danielle's progression is immeasurable, and for that, we will be eternally grateful.

The school had many 'helpers' that carry out any number of tasks, but there was one person who is deserving of a special mention, it is everybody's favourite, Irene, Katie's mum, it would verge on the impossible to even attempt, to give a title to her role within the school, due to the fact, that she pretty much did anything and everything, and she always did it with a smile on her face, everybody loved her.

Now you know when you're little, and you go on a school trip, and are teamed up with someone, a coach buddy. Well, on all those long weekends at Festivals and competitions, Irene was my buddy, when I wasn't busy pressing play on the CD player, I would be sat with Irene, sharing our result predictions.

Danielle had decided relatively early on the College that she wanted to attend, it was Phil Winstons Theatreworks, based in Blackpool, and it was a college with an established history. She had attended a week-long Summer School there, and a 'taster-day', where she had taken lessons alongside the full time students, so when she attended for her audition, she was no stranger to the place.

We had booked a hotel, to stay overnight, the audition day had an early start, I would finish work, pick Danielle up and we would then set off for Blackpool.

Whilst I was still at work, the snow had begun to fall; I was getting a little nervous, we had a 35 mile drive ahead of us that night, we really didn't need this. The snow was getting deeper, I started to question whether I would even manage to get home to pick her up, never mind get her to Blackpool.

In the end, we got there, it took, what seemed like forever, but we made it, through all the snow, finally arriving at the hotel. It has to be said, that night was a very quiet night, Danielle was totally focused, and I expect filled with nervous anticipation, she didn't want to chat, so we didn't, there was no need for pep-talks, words of advice, she was well-prepared, she was ready.

I dropped her off at the college, it was a full day audition, I went back to the hotel, and just sat there, wondering how it was going for her, it has to be said, that day was possibly the longest day of my life, I knew how much this meant to her, sure, we had back-up plans, other colleges that she'd had taster days, but this is the one she wanted.

The last part of the audition, was performing a prepared solo routine in front of Phil Winston himself, I had returned to the college by that point, I was in a room with the other parents, we could hear the tracks playing in the adjoining room, and having prepared the music for her solo, I knew exactly when it was her turn. The door had a small frosted glass pane, and when I heard her song start, I walked over to the door, I couldn't see clearly, but I could make out shapes, I had my fingers crossed, I could feel my heart pounding inside my chest, what I failed to realise;

Was that the glass pane was only frosted on my side, from inside their room; you could see clearly, my face pressed against the glass, peering in!

Following her solo, she was free to leave; Phil had said her solo was 'a beautiful dance'. On the drive home she filled me in on the full events of the day, it seemed to have gone well, and I sensed a quiet confidence in Danielle.

A few days later, and a letter arrived through the letter-box, Danielle was at school, so I had to wait until she was home, to find out if the news held within was to be good or bad.

When she came back home from school, she took the letter upstairs, she later told me that she had got under the duvet to open it, I have no idea why, I waited downstairs, my fingers crossed, it didn't words, I heard the sound of feet, landing on the floor above, as she jumped out of bed, the speed by which those feet were now hurtling downs the stairs, I knew instantly it was good news, great news, the best news!

She smiled at me, running at me, hugging me, one of those really tight hugs, I held her, I was so happy for her, I could feel a tear running down, over my cheek, the dream had just got a little closer.

She spent three years at the college, the course compressed into three days a week, it helped on reducing accommodation and living costs, while giving the student the opportunity to find work on their days off, she had a wonderful time, she made some incredible life-long friends, and she grew, as a person, and as a dancer.

She graduated at the end of those three years with a Diploma in Dance and Musical Theatre, and an IDTA Teaching qualification.

And so, the time had arrived, to move on, to take that final step, to secure that first contract as a professional dancer....

CHAPTER 8 – AUDITIONS

'If you had one shot, or one oppor-
tunity, to seize everything you ever
wanted
In one moment, would you capture it, or just let it slip' **Eminem**

Marshall Bruce Mathers, 'Eminem, without doubt, the greatest and most influential rapper, singer song-writer of all time. Yet, it is in his role as an actor, in the blockbuster movie, '8 mile', that I bring attention to. The scene where he catches the bus to work, he sits solemnly, quiet, fo-cused. Headphones on, his gaze out of the window, looking, but not seeing, distracted, his thoughts elsewhere.

And it reminds me of Danielle, on a car journey to an audition!

Believe me, they are very quiet affairs, the majority of auditions require an early start, now that alone is guaranteed to make for a solemn ambience, and Danielle, in much the same way as in her preparation for her College audition, well, put simply, she prefers not to talk, instead, to concentrate, focus, on the task ahead.

'The first rule of Audition Club is; you don't talk about Audition Club' **Danielle**

Now as you can imagine, very few companies or agents take the decision to hold auditions in little old Oswaldtwislte, I can't imagine why that is, so inevitably auditions always involve travel, usually to a city. At best, that will be Manchester, and at worse, and so very common, London.

For the Manchester auditions, Danielle would often catch the train, or trains to be more exact, Blackburn to Preston, where she could then gat a train in to Manchester, where she might meet up with friends attending the same audition, safety in numbers and all that. Other times, I would drive her, drop her off, sometimes even waiting, until it had finished, and then bringing her back home.

Now the things with auditions, is you can never be really sure how long they will last, yes, they might have an estimated time that the day will finish. But auditions normally take the format of rounds; with cuts made at the end of each one. So, worst case scenario, you take an eternity to get ready, perfecting your make-up, not too much, wanting that 'natural' look, you wear the outfit that you have pondered upon over the last few days, you make the long journey to the venue, then in a blink of an eye, you've been cut at the first round!

Auditions are a harsh process, merciless; I suspect they are the last remaining link to the Roman Empire, and the Gladiators doing battle in the Colosseum, the barbaric, savage entertainment re-enacted in the audition process, with each round of cuts akin to the thrusting of a gladiator's sword into the chest of a defenceless, tired, and starving beast.

In all fairness, as brutal as a first round cut is, it holds no comparison with that fatal blow of the sword, delivered, at the very last step. Having being short-listed, you've done the maths, the numbers game, they need three dancers, and the shortlist is nine people, that's a one in three chance, out of the hundreds that started that audition day. It is when that blow is delivered then, with hope and confidence high, that is when the sword cuts deep, brutal.

But, that is the audition process, always has been, always will be, you just have to get used to it.

Danielle had her fair share of both those outcomes, she came close to some very interesting contracts, cruise ships, production shows abroad, and it always hurt a little more when the rejection came at the final hurdle.

Ktz Dance invited established, professional dancers into the studio, to do workshops with the students, on one occasion, the dancer needed to be picked up from the train station.

It will come as no surprise to you by this point on the book, yes; it was I who adopted that role too.

I insisted on it, it gave me an opportunity, an audience with someone with experience of the industry, someone who could answer some of many of my questions.

On the journey, the girl spoke about a career as a dancer, answering my questions with apparent honesty, to the point that she said, if she were to have a daughter, she would not allow her to pick the route of professional dancer. Now it's possible, I had caught her on a bad day, but in truth, I suppose she was just highlighting the negative side of things, to make me aware, make Danielle aware.

◆ ◆ ◆

Whilst at college, Danielle had started a part-time job, working for a company that hosted themed birthday parties, I say birthday, but in fact, they hosted just about any party. Ironically, as a child, Danielle had a birthday party there, I remember thinking at the time, what a truly innovative idea it was. The party was an amazing success.

Now, years later, and she had started work there, the set-up was incredibly professional, the room décor, the scripts, the characters and the costumes, well they were just so authentic, there seemed no expense spared, no detail overlooked.

They were long, hard, tiring days, but Danielle would always return home with a sweet story or two; a child's reaction, a parents comment, a post on social media, something that made all that hard work worth it.

I think she kind of liked the wage side of things too.

She also worked, for the same company, in a similar role, providing entertainment for birthday parties and special events on location, she enjoyed that side.

I would take her to the location, dropping her off at a strategic point, somewhere I could remain out of sight, and she would arrive at the party and be greeted by all the excited children.

She had to remain in character the entire time, even when interacting with the parents, some of which found it a little strange;

"Thank you so much for today, you've been amazing, my daughter has had the best day, and how will you get home from here?"

Danielle would have to reply, still using the accent of the character;

"Oh my Pumpkin Coach will be along soon"

You can imagine the expression on the mothers face. But it was important, to keep the magic, from walking through the door, to leaving, she was in character. She played a whole host of characters, many of the Disney Princesses, an Enchanted Fairy, and a Christmas Elf.

In the build up to Christmas, they would hire premises in various town centres, and transform them into a place of pure imagination, Lapland. Now don't think this was just your average Santa's Grotto here. These places were absolutely incredible, so much detail, so many different aspects, various rooms, Santa's workshops, televisions mounted on the walls, interactive messages, a host of characters guiding the children around the rooms, all creating a truly immersive experience. One of the characters would lead the children to the penultimate room, a big solid, wooden door at the end, the character would act out a little scene to further enhance the anticipation and excitement, and then the door would open, and there, standing in front of them, would be the man himself, Father Christmas.

Truly magical, as you can imagine, they proved popular, and

in the days preceding Christmas, very busy, it was common for Danielle to work a twelve hour shift, arriving early in the morning, to get into character/costume, there was an array, a fairy, an elf, a toy soldier from the nutcracker. There would be a constant, relentless, flow of children throughout the day, and with late night shopping, came long days. She enjoyed it and the busier the day, the quicker it passed.

Father Christmas, indeed all the characters, were played by 'professional' performers, all highly skilled at their craft, but on one day, they were missing someone to be Father Christmas, and as luck had it, it was my day off!

Yes, I did, I really did, for one day only, I became the most popular man of all time, the one, the only, Santa!

I had lines to learn, a script, I too arrived early that morning, and on the car journey there, I too;

'Sat solemnly, quiet, focused, headphones on, gazing out of the window, looking, but not seeing, distracted, my thoughts elsewhere'

Just as Eminem had, just as Danielle had, on those drives to the audition, I suddenly understood it, as the realisation hit me, the enormity of the pressure that I felt under, the weight of expectation weighing heavily on my shoulders, I was to be Father Christmas, I could not afford to mess this up, I didn't want to be the man that crushed a young child's dreams, ruined the imagination of Christmas.

It seemed to take forever to get ready, I had to have the prosthetic beard glued on, and the suit, the heavy suit, it was so realistic, I swear they had borrowed from the man himself, to be returned in time for the big night itself, I'd better take care of it, just in case.

Once I was ready, I looked in the mirror, I was unrecognisable as myself, for I truly did look like the real Father Christmas, they had completed the most remarkable of transformations with prosthetics, make up and costume.

It was nerve wracking, but it was fun, my partner in the room that day, playing the 'Toy Soldier' was a young, budding actress, Tilly. She took upon herself an extra role that day, the role of my 'carer'. She was wonderful with me, I would stand nervously, in preparation for the next bout of excited visitors, and she would check me over, ensuring every detail was right, my robe, my spectacles, my beard, and as the knock at the door, she would glance over at me and give me a knowing smile, one that instilled confidence in me, and got me through the encounter. I am truly thankful to her for that day, and I hope, one day, when I'm sat watching a TV programme or a movie, her face will pop up on screen, and I will know she has found success. I wish her all the very best in finding that success.

Last Christmas, Danielle was invited to play the character of one of Santa's elves at a special, private Christmas party, hosted by a local TV and Radio presenter, for her young son and his friends.

I drove her to the presenter's house, a few days before the event to discuss the event. She was a lovely lady and invited me to be there to hear the plans, and very elaborate plans they were indeed.

The group of young children were to meet up at a local park, where they would sing Carols, at which point, the elf would make an impromptu appearance, running from inside a small cluster of trees in the centre of the park, she would join them, explaining that she had lost Father Christmas, requesting their assistance to help find him and save Christmas, a treasure trail would ensue, through the park, the streets, that would culminate back at the presenters house, where they would find him.

Now, it was December, cold, frosty, and the park would be dark and isolated, Danielle, obviously, needed to take up her position within the tree area well ahead of any children arriving. It didn't seem the best of ideas to leave her stranded alone in that environment.

Oh come on, you already knew I'd be involved at some point didn't you!

And so, the plan was, I would hide inside the trees, in a body-guard role, Danielle could keep warm, wearing a coat, hat, scarf and gloves over her elf costume. And when we got the cue, she could remove them and set off on her performance. I could stay out of sight, until the group had gone on their merry way through the park, I could then leave the trees and re-join the group further ahead. I couldn't foresee see any problems with that.

> "Can you not Ian? Can you not see the obvious flaw
> to the plan? Crack on then, Good Luck!"

And so, we arrived in good time, we took up our position within the trees, and we awaited the arrival of the guests.

It was a freezing night, temperatures had plummeted, each footstep greeted with the crunching sound of frozen leaves beneath us. As people started to arrive in clusters, we realised, trees in winter, with their leaves abandoned, lay on the floor, are quite transparent, and people were arriving from different directions, causing us to constantly move position, constantly jockeying for a position that would offer us the best coverage. It ended up with us in fits of giggles, and it lightened the mood ahead of the performance.

And so, Danielle received her cue, and off she went, I stayed as planned watching the events unfold, it was an amazing entrance, the children were surprised, excited, and they set off. It was time for me to make a move.

That's the point that I realised the little flaw!

As I stepped from the trees, there I was, a middle-aged man, alone, carrying girls' clothing!

Oh look, dog walkers! There they are, strolling through the park, coming to an abrupt stop, pointing at me!

I should walk over, explain to them, and tell them all about the event.

Is that what you did Ian, no, it's not is it!

I ran!

I did the one thing that would compound my guilt further, leaving the scene of the crime!

I blame the fight or flight reflex, you don't get to choose which, it chooses you.

And so, I re-joined the group on their adventure, it gave me something to do whilst I was waiting for the arrival of the police helicopter overhead, and the impending attack of the police dogs, slowing me down enough to be tasered more effectively.

This was a dream unfolding in front of those children's eyes, as the elf, following the sparkling, fairy dust that the sleigh had left in its mist, rounding the final corner to the house; it was a breath taking vision.

As music boomed from the outdoor speakers, the elf excitedly ran to be re-united with Father Christmas, followed closely, by a hoard of excited children. The garden was decorated to perfection, Santa was sat on his throne in the centre of the garden, and to the side of him was a reindeer, yes a real life reindeer, with antlers, in fact the only thing missing was a red nose.

I watched from a distance, filled with immense pride, as Danielle continued in her role, the children had the best of time, before finally getting in line and taking turns to receive a few private words and a present from Father Christmas.

The event was to continue indoors, but first it was time to say goodbye, and the children all lined up to wave off Santa, the elf and the reindeer. A truly magical night, a successful night,

Danielle was freezing; the Elf costume had offered little in protection against the elements, so I took her home and Pam had a mug of hot chocolate ready for our return, well earned in my opinion.

◆ ◆ ◆

And so, the auditions continued, they say that the hardest contract to achieve, is that first one, the old adage, they want people with experience, but how do you get that experience if nobody gives you that first chance.

Danielle disliked the London auditions the most, they were long arduous journeys, but so many companies hold their only auditions down there.

The journey entailed an overnight coach drive, we would drop her off at Accrington bus station, where she would board the coach and head off to London, arriving around 6 o clock the following morning, a coffee and breakfast in McDonalds, using the facilities to wash and apply make-up, get changed into audition attire, and then a tube ride to whichever studio or theatre, the auditions were being held.

She would audition, before making the reverse journey back home.

I was impressed with her commitment, it would have been easy to shy away from that journey on occasion, to have found an excuse not to do it, but she didn't, she proved resolute, she had a dream and she would do whatever it took to achieve it, and we knew perseverance would pay off, that an opportunity would come.

'Follow your dreams and the Universe will open doors for you, where there were only walls'

During my time working away I met a truly wonderful character, full of his own little quirks, as are we all, but a man who's company I enjoyed every single minute of, he was called Arthur, he was in the Autumn of his career as I was in my spring, he was a constant source of advice, anecdotal tales of trips gone by.

He had a dream, it was a little Del Boy, 'this time next year', but he always told me of his dream, it was to become a millionaire.

To give a little insight into his character, I will share with you, a statement he once made, one that that I found deeply profound, especially coming from him, and his reputation for being, shall we say frugal with his finances.

Sat I a bar one night, we were discussing, putting to rights the way of the world, and he declared in a somewhat prophetic manner, that profound statement;

"If I was the King of England, I would demand that every citizen of this great land be he royalty or a lowly peasant, put all his money, however small or large that sum may be, into a pot, one pot, the same pot. Then that money should be divided back, equally between every person, resulting in everyone having the same amount of money"

I sat, in awe, in disbelief, I had miss-judged this man before me, and I found myself pondering his theory, but before I had chance to ponder long, he finished a particularly long swig of his cold beer, banged the empty glass down onto the wood table, and proudly announced;

"And once I spent mine, I would order we do it all over again"

And the last I heard of him, and this is true, is that he is actually now a millionaire, a combination of working for himself and them wisely investing in his two sons business of designing and landscaping golf courses.

He had a dream, he searched, chased and he persevered, worked hard for that dream, and he found it.

I had fast become like an agent to Danielle, minus the 10% fee, seeking out auditions, opportunities, and upcoming job offers.

I found one such opportunity posted, it was for a company with an upcoming UK tour, performing shows at Theatres nationwide, they were holding an audition for dancers, and the venue was in Leeds, much closer and easier than London. Danielle wanted to attend, initially not entirely sure whether it was something she would want to do, but as she said, it was worth going, to find out more, and it was more audition experience. I was off work that day, so I drove her to Leeds, picking Saffron, her friend from college, up at the train station, before heading to the venue, a dance studio. I dropped them off, wished them luck, the found a space on the car park, where I waited.

'You better lose yourself in the music, the moment

You own it, you better never let it go

You only got one shot, do not miss your chance to blow

This opportunity comes once in a lifetime'

I had parked in a spot that offered a clear view of the front doors. I would know when they had finished a round and made a cut, as dancers would appear though those doors, with that familiar look of disappointment written on their face.

I would sit there, hoping not to see Danielle, and I would know she was through to the next round. My phone would 'ting' and I would look down to find a quick text revealing that fact.

It was a long day; people often ask me why I just sit there, in the car, for hours. Yes, I could got treat myself to a pub lunch, do a little window shopping, have a walk, take in the sights. But the thing is, I can't, I'm too distracted, my thoughts focused solely on the audition, on those doors, and I was exactly where I wanted to be, parked across from those doors. And in truth, the longer I sat there, the more content I was, because that meant things were going well in there.

When the audition was finally over, Danielle returned to the car, I sensed her upbeat mood, and knew instantly things had gone well.

It was Friday, late afternoon, the drive home was busy and long, but it gave her a great opportunity to tell me all about the audition.

She told me it was the most intense audition she had attended so far, that the people seemed really nice, the guy who was announcing the cuts, did so with genuine regret and compassion, taking time to explain to the unlucky ones their reasoning and offering words of encouragement.

He informed the successful ones, left at the end, that they would receive a phone call the following week.

They needed four dancers, and the small number of candidates left at the end, meant Danielle had a fighting chance.

During the next week, she received a phone call from Colin, the guy from the audition, it was he and his partner Marie that owned the company, it was a little like an informal telephone interview, him getting to know Danielle a little better, yes, he had seen her dance, but that wasn't enough, it was important to them to select the 'characters' for this opportunity, they had announced at the audition that they had no room for prima donnas, they wanted a close knit group, with a 'family' feel.

The call had gone well, but Colin had been honest, mentioning that they didn't normally like to take on graduates, citing the obvious reasons. It tempered our confidence a little; the call had ended with him telling Danielle that she would receive a further call tomorrow with a final decision.

One thing you learn with this audition thing, is that there is always waiting, on a phone call, an email, a letter, always waiting.

However, on this occasion, that waiting was cut short, as soon after the phone call, Danielle had received a further one whilst upstairs in her room. She finished the call before running down stairs shouting;

"I got it! Colin's just rang back, they offered me the contract!"

Now, ironically, that was on the day of my 50th birthday, in the preceding weeks I had caused great annoyance and despair amongst my family, they had, obviously hoped to get me a special present to mark the landmark event, but I was proving difficult, offering little in the way of suggestions.

I'll be honest; I'm not good with things like that; fuss, attention, gifts, Danielle will tell you, over the years I have developed a preference for, home-made, sentimental, personal treasures, than expensive, bought items.

And on that special day in August, yes, I was the youngest in the class, my 50th birthday ,my half a century, as Danielle stood before us, making her excited announcement, I looked across the room and realised I had got exactly what I wanted, the best gift in the world, the most special of gifts!

It was a 50" 4K Ultra HD Smart Flat screen TV!

Ok, so it was the news, Danielle's wonderful news, had that been the only present I had received that day, I would have gone to bed that night, happy, and content.

Rehearsals commenced within a short time, Danielle joining the rest of the cast in Sunderland, where they would spend two weeks in intensive rehearsals.

The four dancers shared a house for that time, they would spend long days at a dance studio, initially learning the routines, under the guidance of a successful and renowned choreographer, before cleaning the routines ahead of the opening night.

Just prior to Danielle, making the trip up to Sunderland, she had started with the beginnings of a cold, and whilst there, it developed, she was so ill with it, but had little option but to just carry on regardless. I mentioned previously, regarding Danielle's ability to deal with illness.

Every night, we would FaceTime, I keen to know all the details of the days' rehearsals.

Danielle, keen to tell me all about her symptoms!

I would be asking;

> *"Which section of the show have you been working on today, how did it go?"*

To look down at the screen, and find myself staring down her throat, her mouth, wide open, a close up;

> *"It's really sore, Look at the lumps, it hurts when I swallow"*

I did what I could, what any father would do; I set up a 'Just Giving' fundraising account, an effort to raise enough money to enable us to take her to America for treatment, they had lozenges out there that weren't available over here, it had to be worth a try!

But alas, all efforts were in vain, we failed to raise enough, life can be cruel at times.

I know what you're thinking, how callous, unsympathetic. I agree, I blame my job, but that said, I did make the necessary efforts to obtain a course of antibiotics, that we duly sent up to Sunderland, and within a couple of days, the crisis had been averted.....I'm not all bad!

And so, with rehearsals complete and the show ready, the cast set off on the road, heading to the West Midlands for the opening night at The Core Theatre, Solihull.

The show, *'Rolling Back the Years'* was, to quote;

> *'One of the biggest shows of its kind in the UK; featuring songs, from the 50s. 60s and 70s.*
>
> *This spectacular show is starring West End and International vocalists, supported by the stunning Timeless Showgirls.*
>
> *Beautifully costumed and choreographed for each decade, add to that a touch of comedy, fabulous harmonies and over 160 dazzling costumes.*
>
> *This high energy show is not to be missed!'*

And miss it, we certainly did not, I lost count just how many of those shows we went to, a combination of;

On my own, and with Pam.

Ben, my Mum and Dad, Helen Handshaker, Georgia, Miss J.

My brother Jamie and Niece Teleri, who live down in Plymouth, attending the Exeter Show.

Liv, a fellow dancer from Ktz, and her Mum Elaine, a helper at the school at watched first hand Danielle's progression.

We even tied in a little holiday, the last show was at the Beacon Arts Centre in Greenock, Scotland. Pam's mum joining us for the week and taking in the show.

I mention these people, because I know, just how much it meant to Danielle that they went, made the effort, she would feel an extra buzz on stage when she looked out into the audience and saw a familiar face. She had come a long way, she was proud of her ability, proud of the show she was performing in, proud of the cast she was performing alongside, and she wanted to show all that off. Not just to an audience, but to people who knew her.

After the show, a couple of the cast members would do a 'meet and greet' with the audience. On the occasion that any of the cast had family or friends in the audience, they would be one of them.

We would stand back, allowing Danielle to spend time with the people, saving our own little 'meet and greet' until the end.

I loved just standing there, watching, from afar, as she chatted with them, basking in their adulation, signing autographs, programmes. I got almost as much pleasure from those moments, that I did watching the show.

And those shows were amazing, I would happily go and watch them, even if Danielle wasn't involved, I would recommend that you look them up, find out the next upcoming show, and go enjoy the most wonderful night's entertainment.

Once the audience had left, it was our turn to meet Danielle, and the rest of the cast, of Timeless Theatre Productions.

Colin and Marie, the Producers and Directors of the company, joined on stage by Mike and Jenni, those four together, making up the singers, all bosting amazing voices, complimenting each other well in the harmonies, with Colin and Mike also bringing comedy into the proceedings.

The Timeless Showgirls; made up of two Sarah's, Deanna and our very own Danielle, graced the stage with their wonderful routines, interacting so well with the singers.

Danielle had been very lucky, her first contract, and she was working alongside the most perfect team, they became so close during that tour, and together had the most fantastic time, making and sharing some amazing memories. It was hard, tiring, finishing one show, packing everything away, before making the journey to the next Town, ready for the next show, but it was a good grounding for her, and she had fun doing it.

She had such a good time during that tour, she signed up to do the next one, *'Memory Lane'*, similar in format to *'Rolling Back The Years'*, but with completely new material.

Included in that new material, was a song that Colin performed, and Danielle had drawn attention to it, mentioning it to me prior to us attending on of the shows, that night I listened, possibly a little more intently than I might otherwise have. It is a song written in 1982, by Jeff Silbar and Larry Henley, and originally recorded by Kamahl.

The song gained popularity following the recording in 1988, by actress and singer Bette Midler, for the soundtrack to the film *'Beaches'*

That evening I sat, prepared, and I listened intently, to Colin's beautifully performed rendition of the song.

Now I can't be sure if Danielle simply just liked the song, or Colin's version of it specifically, but as I listened to the words, I began to wonder if there was a message, a sentiment, to those lyrics that meant something to her, one that she was sharing with me.

Now, the original Kamahl track, contained an opening that I've not found on the Bette Midler version, it was a spoken introduction, a narrative, and I'd like to share those words with you first;

"You and I have travelled far together,

And shared so many things, so many memories.

But there are some things that I want you to know, I left unsaid"

And now, those beautiful lyrics;

It must have been cold there in my shadow,
To never have sunlight on your face.
You were content to let me shine, that's your way.
You always walked a step behind.

So I was the one with all the glory,
While you were the one with all the strength.
A beautiful face without a name for so long.
A beautiful smile to hide the pain.

Did you ever know that you're my hero,
And everything I would like to be?
I can fly higher than an eagle,
For you are the wind beneath my wings.

It might have appeared to go unnoticed,
But I've got it all here in my heart.
I want you to know I know the truth, of course I know it.
I would be nothing without you

Oh, the wind beneath my wings.
You, you, you, you are the wind beneath my wings.
Fly, fly, fly away. You let me fly so high.
Oh, you, you, you, the wind beneath my wings.
Oh, you, you, you, the wind beneath my wings.

Fly, fly, fly high against the sky,
So high I almost touch the sky.
Thank you, thank you,
Thank God for you, the wind beneath my wings

Beautiful, meaningful, emotive words.

Could it be that is the reason Danielle highlighted it?

Am I, indeed, the wind beneath her wind, and the one with all the strength that allowed her to be that eagle, to shine? The one with all the glory whilst I went unnoticed in the background.

Unnoticed? In the background?....Ian, you were so ahead of the foreground, you couldn't even see the background from where you were!

Where you in the background when you and your dance dad buddies were shaking your stuff, unnoticed in your starring role as Father Christmas, in the background when you were exposed as the park stalker, running from the tress, unnoticed rocking the ballet on that stage in Rhodes.

You were never really in the background, because you were blessed, lucky, you were stood right beside her, through it all, yes, you might have been a bit of a breeze beneath her wings, but only because she let you, you've been a lucky man in that respect.

I really have, and I know it, and I am truly appreciative of every minute of it.

And so, with two successful UK Tours under her belt, she returned to the audition scene, but this time, with experience, prepared.

It wasn't long before another successful audition led to another contract, this time abroad, a summer contract on the Island of Rhodes.

CHAPTER 9 – ENCORE

"And now, the end is near, and so I face the final curtain"

"Yes, there were times, I'm sure you knew when
I bit off more than I could chew"
"I did It"
"My Way"

I hear you shout, scream, crying out;

"More....More...."

"Please, No More!"

W ell ladies and gentlemen, we have almost reached the end of our journey together, and I have to say, it has been a true pleasure.

It has been, as expected, a real challenge, and those words, from the all-time classic *'My Way'* sum a lot of it up, yes, there have been many times that I've thought that I had overestimated my ability, bitten off more than I could chew.

Not just to write this thing, but to keep going, to the end, and actually finish it, bring it to a conclusion, and now in this final chapter, I am close.

I think you'll agree, I have done it my way, in truth, it's the one way I know, I have no doubt broken many literary rules along the way, not conforming to what is the right and proper way.

And I think that can be said of much of the contents of the book, indeed my life, and my story.

All those opportunities, all those experiences, they were all things I had never done before, they were all firsts. And I did them to what I believe was the best of my ability, granted, I didn't get everything right, but I tried.

Now I've noticed, when people write a book of this nature, like an autobiography, they often contain a section or sections that can be quite shocking, revealing, a confession of some misdemeanour or other.

Having just read Lily Allen's book, I found she was very honest on many things, I loved how honest and frank her words were, it made for an interesting, captivating read, learning much about the person behind the image.

Even the people you'd least expect, David Cameron for example, his recent release confessing all about smoking cannabis when he was at university.

Now call me cynical, but I'm never totally sure if these little confessions are a genuine attempt to bare all, warts and all, or merely an attempt to spark attention, create interest, become serialised-in a popular newspaper and, in turn, increase sales.

Alongside Lilys book, another two of the best autobiographies

I have ever read, belonged to a comedy legend, and firm favourite of mine, Frank Skinner, and Arsenal and England footballer, Tony Adams.

They were both, as with Lily Allens book, incredibly open, honest, revealing accounts.

I wonder if opening their souls up in the books was, a kind of, self-counselling session, a little in the way that Catholic's seek forgiveness when attending confession at Church.

Maybe it was there was of cleaning out the closet, either way, I totally enjoyed and respected their brutal honesty.
I suspect a lot depends on the person, I trust that Lily would fall into that category, along with Frank and Tony, and the ex-prime minister, we'll its better I choose to leave the jury out on that one.

I mean can you really trust a man, who thought the referendum was actually a good idea!

I mean be honest, it was possibly one of the worst ideas ever, up there with some similarly horrendous ones.

To think, even for a minute, that it would prove a success, that people would vote the right way, it showed a complete lack of judgement, just how far away from reality he was, out of touch with what people wanted, it was obvious from the start Ian, I don't like Mondays was never going to work!

Now, if you were hoping for a similarly sordid revelation in this book, I'm sorry to have to disappoint you, I have no tales of drunken, drug fuelled nights of debauchery to fall back on, no sordid stories, involving drugs, orgies or prostitutes. But, following the release of this book and hopes that it might bring with it success and a little fame and fortune, I can but live in hope!

Now, it felt like at that point, the natural thing to have done, was to finish with a little *'winky'* face emoticon, and possibly a *'hahaha'*

It's something I've struggled with all through this book, so many sentences, paragraphs, crying out to be finished off with a relative emoticon, a *'LOL'*, or a million exclamation or question marks.

"What have we done to this wonderful English Language????hahaha lol!!!!!"

I mean if I wanted to send a message or post on social media, the news that I'm on holiday, that it's warm and sunny, does there really exist a need to add an emoticon of the sun, just for those who don't know what the sun looks like, I mean surely we all know what the sun looks like, well, apart from the good people of Scotland of course.

The other way it has affected me, has been when writing a text, now it's normally such a clinical, speedy affair, but now, I find myself pondering, looking for better wording, a witty aside, checking the spelling and grammar.

"Really Ian, do you now!"

"So why the bloody hell, haven't you done all that when writing this book?"

So now, what about life after this book, what chapters will be writing themselves in the future.

As I said earlier, having just celebrated our 25Th Silver Wedding Anniversary, we will carry on, as a formidable team, heading, making our way to the next milestone, with the children getting older, we will be granted more time together, to do the things we've not been able to do in recent years.

Ben has just started his final year at school, preparing for his turn at those GCSE's, as for after that, well he's a little Egg and Chips himself, unsure of exactly what he wants to do, to become.

Experience has taught me, he will make the right decision, but only when he's good and ready, only once he knows himself.

But he's growing up fast, he's taller than me now, stronger, needless to say, the play-fighting sessions have stopped, he'd kill me nowadays. I look back with great fondness, on the time when we had our little 'boys club', the two of us the only 'select' members, the bedroom door adorned with 'keep out' signs, posters, warnings.

They grow up fast, I knew they would, and that is why I took the time, to enjoy, savour, all those little moments.

What does the future hold for Danielle, well career-wise, she will soon be returning from Greece, she has a short time at home, before flying out, to perform in a show, a short tour of India, and an exciting opportunity indeed.

After that, we don't know, and that is the beauty, and the downside, of her career choice, she will never really know what the future holds. She will just have to go and live it, enjoy it.

And for me, TheMusicIan, I don't know, will this book prove a success, will it make publication, I have no way of knowing, but I have achieved the outcome I set out to do, and that was to write it, and now, having achieved that, sadly it has come time for us to part company.

◆ ◆ ◆

Thank you for taking the time to accompany me on my journey down Memory Lane, I hope you have had as much fun reading it, as I have had writing it.

Now the time has come;

"And so I face the final curtain"
"My friend, I'll say it clear"
I'll state my case, of which I'm certain"

"Join me now, in taking a bow, a curtsy"

As those big, red velvet curtains close on our time together, our journey, my book

◆ ◆ ◆

Acknowledgements

For my mum and dad, who made me the person, the dad, I am today, truly inspirational parents.

For Pam and Ben, for believing in me and for allowing me the time to experience the whole 'dance dad' journey, for supporting me in all of the mad cap adventures, the Dads Dance Army, TheMusician and of course, the writing of this book.

For Danielle, for allowing me to walk beside her, to share all those amazing opportunities, and for creating the best memories along the way.

Katie Readman – Ktz Dance School

Miss J – Roberts Morgan School of Dance

Dance Dads Army -
Andy Fielding
Andy Beaghan
Brett Alderson
Scott Hill
Chris Harrington

Printed in Poland
by Amazon Fulfillment
Poland Sp. z o.o., Wrocław

54584548R00127